Niamh Carty

THE OXFORD
SCHOOL HARMONY COURSE

BOOK II

THE OXFORD SCHOOL HARMONY COURSE

BOOK II

BY

JAMES DENNY

LONDON
OXFORD UNIVERSITY PRESS
NEW YORK TORONTO

Oxford University Press, Walton Street, Oxford OX2 6DP

LONDON   OXFORD   GLASGOW   NEW YORK
TORONTO   MELBOURNE   WELLINGTON
IBADAN   NAIROBI   DAR ES SALAAM   CAPE TOWN
KUALA LUMPUR   SINGAPORE   JAKARTA   HONG KONG   TOKYO
DELHI   BOMBAY   CALCUTTA   MADRAS   KARACHI

ISBN 0 19 317203 8

© Oxford University Press 1961

First published 1961
Sixth impression 1979

Printed in Great Britain by offset lithography by
Billing & Sons Ltd, Guildford, London and Worcester

CONTENTS

INTRODUCTION TO BOOK II

PART III—MORE ADVANCED HARMONY

23 SECONDARY SEVENTHS I

24 THE CHORDS OF THE NINTH AND THEIR DERIVATIVES 6

25 THE CHORD OF THE DOMINANT ELEVENTH 14

26 THE CHORDS OF THE DOMINANT THIRTEENTH 16

27 THE DOMINANT CHORDS OF THE DOMINANT 18

28 THE TRIAD ON THE FLATTENED SUPERTONIC 22

29 THE CHORDS OF THE AUGMENTED SIXTH 29

30 MULTIPLE SUSPENSIONS 36

31 CHANGING NOTES: ACCENTED PASSING NOTES: PEDAL-POINTS: CHROMATIC DECORATION IN PART-WRITING 41

32 HARMONIC RHYTHM AND CHORD RECOGNITION 55

33 MORE ADVANCED MODULATION AND HARMONIZATION IN FOUR PARTS 66

34 MORE ADVANCED CONTRAPUNTAL WRITING IN TWO AND THREE PARTS 73

35 HARMONIZATION OF CHORALES IN THE STYLE OF J. S. BACH 85

APPENDIX C.   WRITING FOR STRINGS 93

APPENDIX D.   WRITING FOR THE PIANOFORTE 103

NOTES: I.   SCALES AND MODES 110

2.   CADENCES 114

3.   FIGURED BASS 121

4.   FORBIDDEN CONSECUTIVES 123

5.   TIME-SIGNATURES 125

DICTATION EXERCISES FOR CHAPTERS 10-21 128

INDEX OF QUOTATIONS 138

INTRODUCTION

Within the limits of this Course it is impossible to discuss advanced harmony in any detail. Instead, the aim of Part III is to acquaint the pupil with the existence of the higher chords of diatonic harmony and to dwell, briefly, on the underlying principles of chromatic harmony. The remaining chapters are concerned with aspects of harmonic and contrapuntal writing which should be familiar to a senior pupil seeking entrance to the university, or intending to take music as a main subject at a college of education.

Before working more advanced exercises, pupils may benefit by reading appendices C and D—on writing for strings and for the pianoforte. It may also help them if they will turn once again to the appendix (in Book I) on conventions in writing music manuscript.

The Notes printed here refer, properly, to the relevant chapters in Book I; but they may still have interest and value for the more mature student.

To the Pupil

Re-read the lines addressed to you in the Introduction to Book I of this Course. The advice given then still applies. But you have now reached the stage at which your own free compositions are possibly of greater value than the short exercises at the end of each chapter. As you learn about fresh chords, try to introduce them at appropriate moments into your own writing. Additional progressions are additional resources at your command.

Be as curious as possible about the means by which the great composers gain their effects. When looking at music, keep your eyes open for instances of the diatonic and chromatic chords discussed in this Book. While listening to music—to whatever music comes your way—keep your ear alert; do what you can to follow modulations from and to the original key; try to identify the steps by which such modulations are carried out. Aural training is important at this point of your studies; apply your skill in this respect to your writing, and to your music listening.

ACKNOWLEDGEMENTS

Acknowledgements are due to the following for permission to quote extracts from the works listed: Boosey & Hawkes Ltd. (Béla Bartók, *Mikrokosmos*); Curwen Edition (Gustav Holst, *The Planets*); Durand & Cie. (Claude Debussy, String Quartet and *Pelléas et Mélisande*, and Camille Saint-Saëns, *Danse Macabre*); Stainer & Bell Ltd. (Gustav Holst, ' Funeral Hymn ' from the *Rig Veda*).

PART III
MORE ADVANCED
HARMONY

23. SECONDARY SEVENTHS

Root Position

1. Chords of the seventh built on any degree of the diatonic scales, except that of the dominant, are termed secondary sevenths. They may be in either major or minor keys. The following are the secondary sevenths in C major:

Fig. 315

I⁷   II⁷   III⁷   IV⁷   VI⁷   VII⁷

2. You will see that II⁷, which we discussed in Chapters 20 and 21, is a secondary seventh. Note that I⁷ and IV⁷ contain major sevenths, while the remainder (like that on the dominant) have minor sevenths.

3. In your **own** writing the sevenths of these chords should, whenever possible, be prepared—just as we learned to prepare suspensions. You will sometimes see an example of an unprepared seventh (as in Fig. 316), but preparation in the regular manner is more common and, until you are used to these chords, simpler. There is one important difference between a suspension and the sounding of a secondary seventh: the former should only be struck on a strong beat, but the latter can be introduced on either a strong or a weak beat.

Fig. 316

Bach

G I⁶ VI⁷ V⁶₅   IV⁷ V

Fig. 317

Allegro

Corelli

(2 Vlns.)

(continuo)

E I⁶ VI⁷ II⁷   V⁷ I⁷ IV⁷ II⁶   V⁷

4. As in the case of II⁷ and V⁷, the seventh should resolve downwards by step, either directly or after touching another harmony note. There is an exception with the (major) sevenths of I⁷ and IV⁷; these may rise, if the circumstances warrant it, while the bass will fall a third.

5. It is often convenient to sound all four notes of a secondary seventh (as in Figs. 316 and 318); but if one has to be omitted, let it be the fifth. If a note must be doubled, let it be the root or third in preference to the fifth. The seventh clearly cannot be doubled.

6. The bass of secondary sevenths in root position will usually follow the recommendations for root progressions given in Chapter 10. Thus, a rise of a fourth is in some cases preferable to a rise of one degree. This applies to I⁷, II⁷ and III⁷. But IV⁷ moves more smoothly to V, V⁷ or II⁶ than to VII. VI⁷ can move equally easily to II, II⁷ or to the first inversion of the dominant seventh, ⁶₅. With VII⁷ the effect is equally good if it moves to I or III.

7. Secondary sevenths in a minor key are, like triads, affected by both the ascending and the descending forms of the melodic minor scale. In C minor the complete series will be:

Fig. 320

I 7 asc.   I 7 desc.   II 7 asc.   II 7 desc.   III 7 asc.   III 7 desc.   IV 7 asc.   IV 7 desc.

V 7 desc.   VI 7 asc.   VI 7 desc.   X   VII 7 asc.   X   VII 7 desc.

8. Of these, both the forms of VII⁷ with the raised sixth degree are unsuitable for your use as they have no reasonable resolution within the tonic key. Of the remainder, the components of each chord should be resolved in the normal manner—raised leading notes rising by step, sevenths and flattened sixths falling. With these principles in mind we can resolve these sevenths as follows:

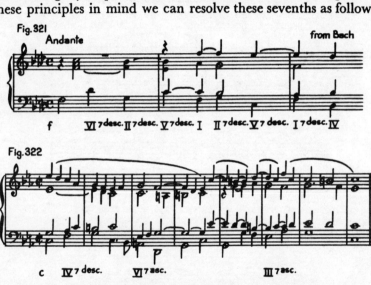

Fig. 321

Andante   from Bach

f   VI 7 desc. II 7 desc. V 7 desc. I   II 7 desc. V 7 desc. I 7 desc. IV

Fig. 322

c   IV 7 desc.   VI 7 asc.   III 7 asc.

9. A succession of secondary sevenths in root position forms the outline of many of the sequences which are a feature in early eighteenth-century composition; examples are at Figs. 317 and 321. While such passages can remain in the tonic key, there are opportunities at every step for modulation (Fig. 318). When using these chords (singly or in pairs) in your own writing, remember that II⁷ is the most common of the series; followed by the sevenths on IV and VI. III⁷ and VII⁷ are more rare.

10. Should the position of a chord produce a diminished seventh from the bass, the figuring will read ⌐7.

Exercises

1. Add alto and tenor parts.

2. Add three parts above.

The Inversions of Secondary Sevenths

11. Of the three possible inversions to each chord of the seventh, the first is that most frequently employed. The figuring of each inversion corresponds with that of the dominant seventh. Do not try to learn the peculiarities and contexts of all inversions of all possible sevenths. Instead, select one or two chords and learn how to use them. Extemporize short phrases at the piano which incorporate the chord, and position, of your choice.

Exercises

3. Add three parts above.

4. Analyse the passage at Fig. 324, naming the key to which each chord belongs.

24. THE CHORDS OF THE NINTH AND THEIR DERIVATIVES

1. We have already seen that a dominant triad in root position can be the basis of a new chord if an additional third is added (that is, a seventh from the bass). In the chapters which follow we shall examine briefly the chords resulting from adding a ninth (major or minor) to the dominant seventh; next, an eleventh; and lastly, a thirteenth (major or minor). These additions complete the series of chords which can be built on the dominant triad by adding successive thirds.

2. This chapter concerns the dominant ninths and the chords derived from them. Reference is also made to the secondary ninths.

3. Since a dominant ninth has five notes, at least one of them must be omitted in four-part writing. If the root is present (in the bass) try to preserve the third and the seventh, since both these

notes combine with the ninth to give this chord its peculiar quality. The fifth will usually be omitted.

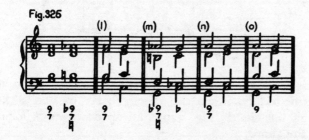

Fig.325

4. Compare (l) and (m) above, in which the fifth is omitted, with (n) which lacks the third, and (o) which has no seventh. While either the third or seventh may have to be left out in three-part writing and in other special circumstances, such omissions in four parts may produce a bare effect.

5. Though at first you will be wise to place the ninth in the top part, there is no rule against its being sounded by an inner one (Figs. 326 and 327). Experience will show you what does and does not sound well.

Fig.326
Adagio assai   Beethoven

Fig.327
Allegro (più moto)   Schubert

6. The examples given so far illustrate the progression of the dominant ninth to the tonic. The bass of the dominant chord can equally well move upwards by step to the submediant or remain stationary while the ninth resolves on to the octave.

Fig. 328

7. Though the most common movement of the ninth itself is downwards by step, it can also effectively rise by step to the third (tenth) of the chord (Fig. 329) or leap downwards to another note of the chord.

Fig. 329
Adagio
Bizet

8. Since the root must be sounded in the bass if the chord is to have its characteristic dissonant quality, inversions of this chord are uncommon. For our present purposes they may be ignored. But the omission of the root altogether provides us with a new chord which is not an inversion but a derivative. You will see from (l) in Fig. 330 that the omission of the root (G) of the major ninth of C leaves us with the secondary seventh, VII⁷. It matters little whether the context suggests that this chord is a secondary seventh or a chord of the ninth with the root omitted; what is important is that by either description the chord belongs to C major.

Fig. 330

9. Similarly, at (m) in Fig. 330 the chord of the minor ninth remaining after the removal of the root can be described as VII⁷ ᵃˢᶜ with a diminished seventh—a secondary seventh in C

minor. It can resolve on to the tonic triad. But this chord has certain characteristics which are important. (*i*) It is composed of three minor thirds—that is, its four notes are equidistant within the octave. (*ii*) The bottom and top notes form a diminished seventh, from which it takes its name.

The Chord of the Diminished Seventh:

Fig. 331

10. At Fig. 331 (l) and (m), this chord is treated as a normal derivative of the dominant. But it can also be a point of modulation.

11. Thus, we know that if the A♭ of the diminished seventh in C minor is lowered to G, a first inversion of the dominant seventh of C minor will result (Fig. 332 (l)). No modulation has been made. But if, instead of treating the A♭ as the ninth, we choose the B♮ and lower it a semitone, then we are changing the root from G to B♭ and so effecting a modulation to (in this case) the key of E♭ ((m), (n) and (o)). But in making this choice the B♮ becomes C♭—the minor ninth above the new root.

Fig. 332

12. We can, in turn, treat the remaining two notes of this chord as the minor ninth and so modulate to two further keys. Some notes must be differently named to establish the old chord in the new key. When the F is regarded as the ninth—that is, when the modulation is to be to A minor—then the root will become E, and A♭ must be changed enharmonically to G♯ (Fig. 333 (p) and (q)). And, finally, when the D is to be the ninth, the root

will be C♯ and two notes must be re-named to conform to the diatonic scale of F♯ (major or minor)—A♭ to G♯, and F♮ to E♯ (r).

Fig. 383

13. Paras. 11 and 12 show that the diminished seventh, in addition to belonging to the approach key, can (as a means of modulation) become diatonic in three other keys: the flattened mediant (of the approach key), the sharpened subdominant, and the submediant. Because of the presence of the minor ninth there will be a strong bias towards minor tonality; but it is equally possible to establish major tonality. Try extemporizing passages on the piano which include the chord of the diminished seventh; first, without modulation; then (by lowering the ninth) modulating to the three possible keys ((l) and (m) below).

Fig. 334

14. But the lowering of the ninth in the diminished seventh is only one method of modulating with this chord. We can also raise three notes a semitone and so convert the remaining (stationary) note into the root of the dominant seventh of a new key. Fig. 335

15. And, thirdly, the two notes comprising the diminished seventh itself can move outwards to form the dominant (in octaves) of a new key. Fig. 336 shows the progressions involved.

Fig. 336

16. There are many ways in which the chord of the diminished seventh can be used. The purpose of this chapter is to bring some of the more important possibilities to your notice rather than to persuade every young composer that harmonic salvation lies in the diminished seventh. Many composers have hardly used the chord at all—and certainly not for modulating; others, like Bach and Beethoven, regarded it as an harmonic 'colour' which appealed to them; it became an integral part of their style of writing. Some quotations are given below of how the diminished seventh has been used in classical writing. (You should also note Chapter 27, para. 3.)

Fig. 337

Andante   Bach

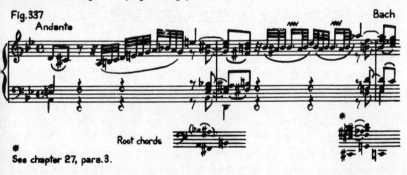

Root chords

✻
See chapter 27, para. 3.

Fig. 338

Allegro   Mozart

Fig. 339

Allegro molto   Beethoven

cresc.

Root chords

Fig. 340   Fig. 341   Wagner
Langsam   Wagner   Mässig langsam   Wagner

Secondary Ninths

17. In theory there is a series of secondary ninths as complete as
their equivalent sevenths. In practice, many of these ninths can
be analysed more satisfactorily as derivatives of other chords. If
the ninth and seventh in Fig. 392 are treated as appoggiaturas,
the resulting chord is nothing more complex than the first
inversion of a triad. Do not try too hard to introduce these chords
into your own writing at present. It is sufficient that you should
know of their existence. (See Fig. 354.)

Exercises

1. Add three parts below. (Opportunities to introduce a chord
of the ninth or diminished seventh are marked.)

Ex. I.

2. Add three parts above.

Ex.2

3. Begin as given and modulate in a few chords to the key named.

Ex.3.

25. THE CHORD OF THE DOMINANT ELEVENTH

1. The eleventh above the dominant is the tonic of the key. As an eleventh is also the compound interval of the fourth, it frequently falls by step to the leading note.

2. The full chord having six notes, at least two must be omitted in four-part writing. When the eleventh is to fall one degree the leading note will be omitted; and either the ninth or the fifth will also be absent. The seventh is usually present. The root, too, is commonly included unless the chord is based on its fifth, in which case it will be the supertonic seventh (II^7) which we discussed in Book I.

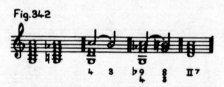

Fig. 342

3. But the eleventh can also rise; in which case the fifth will be omitted and, probably, the seventh and ninth will be present (Fig. 345 (ii)).

4. A distinction should be made between II^7 (in which there is no sign of the dominant of the key) and the second inversion of the dominant eleventh (of which the dominant is an integral part). Compare the following.

Fig. 343   "Wareham"   Fig. 344

5. The eleventh is sometimes prepared as if it were an ordinary fourth above the dominant (Fig. 343). But not infrequently it is unprepared and has the character of an appoggiatura.

Fig. 345
(i)   (ii)

6. For the purpose of analysis you should be aware of the **dominant** eleventh and some of its (rare) inversions. But for your own writing, it is sufficient at this stage to know of the root position and the second inversion, together with the supertonic seventh and its inversions.

Exercises

Add three parts above.

Ex.
(i)

(ii)

(iii)

26. THE CHORDS OF THE DOMINANT THIRTEENTH

1. The most common form of these seven-note chords includes only the root, third, seventh, and (as the topmost note) the thirteenth. The thirteenth itself (either major or minor) resolves one step downwards on to the fifth of the dominant (Fig. 346), or is free to interrupt its resolution by leaping to another harmony note (Fig. 347).

Fig. 346

Fig. 347   Wagner

2. The dominant thirteenth has a rich effect in cadences. Verdi's frequent use of it in such contexts is a feature of his writing. (See also Fig. 108 in which it appears at an unusually low pitch.)

Fig. 348   Verdi
— que spem de — di ——————— sti.

Fig. 349   Verdi

Sup-pli-can-ti par-ce De — — — — us.

Fig. 350   Verdi

3. But this chord is not exploited by the later Romantics only. There are many examples in Beethoven and Schubert. (The quotation in Fig. 352 shows the dominant thirteenth in its first inversion.)

Fig. 351   Adagio   Beethoven

Fig. 352   Molto adagio   Beethoven

Fig. 353   Schubert

(l)   (m)

4. If the root and leading note are omitted from the chord of
the dominant thirteenth we are left with a secondary ninth on
the supertonic (Fig. 354). In such a context the thirteenth (now
the ninth above the supertonic) can satisfactorily be placed in
an inner part; but the supertonic character is now so strong that
any feeling of dominant origin has disappeared.

5. To go a step further and omit the original fifth of the dominant
thirteenth as well as the root and third is only to strip the chord
to IV⁷. By now it has become impossible to claim that the chord
is in any way connected with the dominant. If IV⁷ is not a
chord in its own right (which, as a secondary seventh, it can
claim to be) then the ear will ascribe its origin to the supertonic
(as a derivative of II⁹) rather than to the dominant.

CHROMATIC HARMONY

Our studies up to this point have been concerned with diatonic
harmony. That is, we have examined the structure and use of
chords which belong strictly to the prevailing key. Chords
foreign to the original tonic have only been introduced in the
course of, or after, modulation to another key.
The three chapters which follow are devoted to simple
chromatic harmonies. A chromatic chord is one which is foreign
to the prevailing key and yet is used within it without the
intention of effecting a modulation.

27. THE DOMINANT CHORDS OF THE DOMINANT

1. The title of this chapter is perhaps the clearest explanation
of the *major* supertonic triad and its seventh, ninth, eleventh and

thirteenth as additions to the diatonic harmony of a given key. For example, the chord of A major in Fig. 355 is foreign to the key of G minor. As there is no intention of effecting or implying a modulation, its function in this phrase is that of a chromatic supertonic triad.

Fig. 355

2. Chromatic chords on the supertonic (having, remember, a major third) can be used in minor keys, though they are more frequently to be found in major passages. The first inversion of the triad is more common, and often sounds more gracious, than the root position. The same applies to the chromatic supertonic seventh, for the first and third inversions are more effective than the root position or second inversion. The individual notes of these chords resolve in a manner similar to their dominant equivalent. But note, in Fig. 357, that the sharpened subdominant (the bass note of the first inversion of the chromatic seventh) can effectively descend a semitone to form the bass of the third inversion of the dominant seventh.

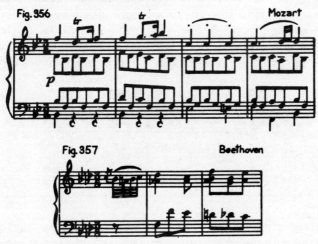

Fig. 356   Mozart

Fig. 357   Beethoven

Fig.358

Brahms

3. While a major or minor ninth can be added above the chromatic supertonic triad or seventh, the most common derivative is the diminished seventh on the sharpened subdominant—that is, a chromatic supertonic minor ninth with the root omitted. Bach uses this chord in both major and minor cadences (Figs. 359 and 360).

Fig.359   Bach Fig.360   Bach

4. The true nature of the chromatic supertonic eleventh and thirteenth is elusive and we are more often left with the impression that a simpler chromatic chord has been embellished with an appoggiatura. If we re-write Fig. 355, do we readily recognize the suspended D in Fig. 361 as a supertonic chromatic eleventh? Or the marked chord in Fig. 362 as the equivalent thirteenth? Probably not. And no great harm will arise if we analyse both chords as ornamented versions of the supertonic chromatic seventh.

Fig.361   Fig.362

5. But supertonic chromatic thirteenths do exist—unmistakably There is one in the sixth bar of Fig. 363, and another in the second bar, with the (minor) ninth in the bass.

Exercises

1. Add parts for alto and tenor.

2. Add three parts above.

28. THE TRIAD ON THE FLATTENED SUPERTONIC

1. Not all chromatic harmony dates from the nineteenth century, however widely it may have been exploited during that period. Its foundations were laid very much earlier. We have seen that Bach made free use of triads and sevenths on the supertonic; he and his contemporaries of the eighteenth century also employed the major triad on the *flattened* supertonic—though even this chromatic chord was inherited from a previous generation.

2. The triad on the flattened[1] supertonic ($\flat$II) has, broadly, two functions. (*i*) As a chromatic triad within an established key, in which context its colour is unmistakable when added to diatonic harmony. (*ii*) As a means of modulating, since any major triad can, in theory, be chosen to represent the flattened supertonic of a new tonality. This chord can occur within, and can be used to approach, both major and minor keys—though its constituent notes lend themselves more readily to the latter.

[1] Though it is convenient to think of the supertonic in this context as being flattened in some keys (e.g., B, f$\sharp$, C$\sharp$) the description will be $\natural$II.

3. Within an existing key, it is unusual to find this triad in root position. But if the context should call for that position, then (in quitting) the root will either fall to the dominant or move by a diminished third to the leading note (Figs. 364 and 376); at the same time the fifth will resolve on to the dominant, following the normal path of the flattened submediant.

Fig. 364

4. The triad on the flattened supertonic is most commonly met with in its first inversion—the so-called Neapolitan sixth. On quitting it, the bass may rise to the dominant (as the foundation of some chord of V, or I$^6_4$); or it can rise a semitone to form the bass of a chord of the diminished seventh (Figs. 365, 368 and 369). The third of ♭II^6 is free to rise or fall but (as in the case of the root position) it will more usually behave as if it were the flattened submediant. If the bass moves to the dominant, the root may resolve on to the tonic or fall by a diminished third to the leading note (see also para. 3). If you extemporize on the piano short phrases which include the Neapolitan sixth within the established key, you will find that the diminished third between the flattened supertonic and the leading note is a characteristic feature. The general outlines of the use of this chord are as follows:

Fig. 365

5. Study the four quotations given below in which the Neapolitan sixth appears as a chromatic chord within the established key. In Fig. 369 (bar 10), ♭II^6 follows the triad of the flattened submediant as part of an interrupted cadence: had the interrup-

tion been on the *raised* submediant the sounding of a Neapolitan sixth would have created an unpleasant false relation—test this yourself by playing these two chord sequences in any key of your choice.

(*i*) I^6_4 V^7 | $\flat VI$ $\flat II^6$ (*ii*) I^6_4 V^7 | VI $\flat II^6$

Fig. 366   Bach

Fig. 367   Bach

Fig. 368   Handel

But there was no man | nei-ther found He an-y   to   com-fort Him.

Fig. 369   Beethoven

6. The second inversion of ♭II is not unknown. Its fifth (the bass in this instance) can conveniently resolve direct on to the dominant or (as in Fig. 370) become the bass of an augmented sixth (see Chapter 29).

Fig. 370

7. In a passage which modulates, the Neapolitan sixth can be treated as the point at which the old tonality gives place to the new. But we can either sound the Neapolitan sixth of the old key —and then quit it as (say) the subdominant of the new (Fig. 371); or we can proceed in our established key until, on arriving on (the first inversion of) a *major* triad, we elect to treat it as ♭II⁶ of a new key (Fig. 372).

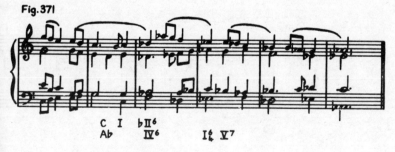

Fig. 371

Fig. 372

8. Since only a major triad (in an established key) can be regarded as the Neapolitan sixth of a new, the number of keys which can be approached in this manner is limited to three from a major key—VII, ♯IV, and III; and two from a minor key—V (through ♭VI) and, less satisfactorily, II (through III^{desc.}) (Figs. 373 and 374).

Fig. 373

9. Just as dominant chords of the dominant can belong to a given key (Chapter 27), so ♭II and the Neapolitan sixth of the dominant can be regarded as chromatic chords within an established key. In Fig. 375 the chord of B♭ is approached and quitted as dVI since the tonality of D minor remains undisturbed by the chromatic supertonic seventh which follows. But the quotation from Beethoven is modulating to A minor, and so dVI is, more logically, quitted as a♭II.

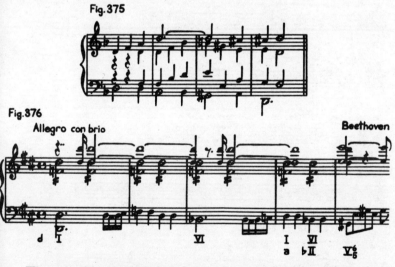

10. Though this chapter has been concerned with major triads on the flattened supertonic, minor triads can also appear on that degree. They are rare and, for the present, should be observed rather than written. A beautiful example in root position is quoted below from Schubert: it resolves on to an augmented sixth (Chapter 29) before reaching a cadential six-four.

Fig. 377

Adagio

Schubert

Exercises

1. Add three parts below.

Ex.1

(i)

(ii)

(iii)

(iv)

2. Add three parts above.

Ex.2

(i)

(ii)

3. Begin as given and modulate to the key named by means of the triad on the flattened supertonic.

Ex.3

29. THE CHORDS OF THE AUGMENTED SIXTH

1. The augmented sixth, the last in our survey of chromatic chords, exists in three forms—the French, the Italian, and the

German sixths. Fig. 378 shows all three as they appear in C major (or minor), together with simple resolutions.

Fig. 378

French   Italian   German

2. All three forms have the flattened sixth degree of the scale as their bass—a reminder that they resolve most naturally on to the dominant of the key and not on to the tonic. Yet if the flattened submediant derives from a dominant root, the leading note of the dominant has its root on the supertonic, thus suggesting that the chord of the augmented sixth has two roots. A glance at Fig. 379 will make this clear—though it is an explanation of origin rather than an aid to the use of this chord.

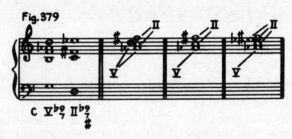

Fig. 379

3. The French sixth has a distinctive quality as it is the only form containing the interval of a whole tone. This gives it a greater pungency, if not thickness of tone, than the others. In resolving, the augmented sixth will expand to an octave on the dominant (Fig. 378); the inner parts will move so as to form I$^6_4$ or V (Fig. 380).

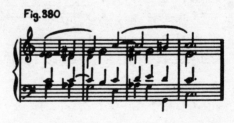

Fig. 380

Fig. 381

4. The Italian sixth lacks the supertonic which is present in the
French form. The fact that it is composed of only three notes
accounts for a greater transparency in tone-quality. In four-part
writing, only the third can be doubled (though this does not rule
out doubling in an orchestral score).

Fig. 382

5. A passing note can convert an Italian sixth into a French
sixth. The change is more noticeable at a slow tempo (Fig. 383).
There is no harm in such a progression; but it is better to increase
complexity or thickness of texture (as in this case) than to do the
reverse.

Fig. 383

6. Lastly, the German sixth, the most commonly used of the three forms. The outward movement of the two parts forming the augmented sixth is still the ruling factor in quitting this chord; but a direct move to the dominant may create consecutives. Fig. 378 shows a resolution on to I$^c_4$. It is not uncommon for the sharpened leading note of the dominant to fall a semitone and so become the subdominant of the tonic (as at Figs. 385 and 386).

7. Though approach to the augmented sixth is frequently and conveniently made by the outward movement of the extreme parts, the bass has considerable freedom in this regard.

8. The chords of the augmented sixth have many inversions. That which you will come across most often is the third inversion

of the German form. One example is at Fig. 387. Another instance, which has a strange effect, is quoted from Saint-Saëns. The dance, of which this quotation is a part, is firmly in G minor when it is interrupted by the horns sounding, and holding, the flattened submediant; after 'cockcrow' on the oboe (which emphasizes the chord of E flat), the ear hears a heavy chord on the strings which might be interpreted as V_2^4 (bass on D flat) of A flat major. But not until ten bars later, when a resolution is made on to I_4^6 of G minor, is it shown that D flat has never existed, and that a low C♯ (as the leading note of the dominant) was the bass of the third inversion of the German sixth of G minor. (Compare this progression with that in Fig. 528.)

Fig. 387

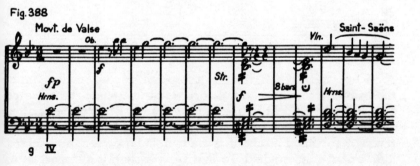

Fig. 388

9. The possibility of renaming components of the German sixth and converting this chord into the dominant seventh of a new key is an important aid to modulation. An example at Fig. 389 shows how V^7 of D major becomes the German sixth of D flat. Beethoven (Fig. 390) makes an approach with V^7 of B major, converts it enharmonically into a German sixth and so modulates into B flat major.

Fig. 389

Sehr feierlich

Wagner

Fig. 390

Allegro vivace

Beethoven

six bars then:-

10. Since the French sixth is composed of two major thirds the bass of either can be regarded as the flattened sixth degree of a given key. So here is another method of modulation: after arriving on a French sixth the two thirds can be enharmonically reversed so that the chord is quitted in a key an augmented fourth above the original. In Fig. 391 the sixth is approached in C minor and quitted in F♯ minor.

Fig. 391

(i)   (ii)

11. You should distinguish in your mind between the chord of the augmented sixth (especially in its Italian form) and (*i*) the first inversion of the triad on the leading note of a major key, and (*ii*) VII⁶ in the mode on E, when it forms part of the Phrygian cadence.[1] A glance at Figs. 524, 525, etc., will show that a chord of the sixth bears no resemblance to the augmented sixth, yet in looking at musical scores confusion is all too possible between them.

Exercises

1. Add alto and tenor parts. (Chords of the augmented sixth are figured.)

Ex.1

[1] See Note on Cadences.

2. Analyse the above exercises, noting the modulations and the means by which they are effected.

30. MULTIPLE SUSPENSIONS

1. In Chapter 15 we considered single suspended or retarded notes. But study of the higher dominant chords will have shown you that more than one note can be suspended at a time—as, for example, $\frac{9}{7}$ falling to $\frac{8}{6}$; and it is not uncommon to find two or more notes suspended simultaneously.

Fig. 392

2. The three 'true' suspensions in diatonic harmony are those of the fourth, seventh, and ninth. From the quotation given above it is clear that $\frac{9}{7}$ is a satisfactory combination: $\frac{9}{4}$ is equally so. A minor seventh and a fourth are sometimes suspended in a decorated version of the medieval cadence (Fig. 516); but in contexts later than 1500 this combination is usually attributable to the decoration of a $\frac{7}{3}$ or $\frac{6}{4}$ (Fig. 394) and can hardly be termed a double suspension.

Fig. 393

Fig. 394

Fig. 395

3. Further combinations can be between a suspension and a retardation: $^{\sharp7}_{4} - ^{8}_{3}$ or $^{9}_{\sharp7} - 8$ (Fig. 396). When these appear at cadences it is usual for the suspended notes to be re-struck at the point of dissonance: the result can sometimes be analysed as an appoggiatura.

Fig. 396

4. If we go a step further and suspend three or more notes we find that such multiple suspensions are usually the combination of one or more 'true' suspensions with either (i) retarded notes or (ii) notes which, on suspension, are not dissonant with the bass. The simplest example of (ii) is the suspended six-four in which only the fourth is a discord—though the affinity between these two notes prompts the sixth to resolve in parallel with the fourth as if it were itself a discord.

Fig. 397

Fig. 398

5. Study the following quotations. Take note of the direction in which the individual parts move: that 9, 7, and 4 and the flattened 6 move downwards (as we expect): and that 7 (especially if it is the leading note), 5, and 2 may move upwards.

Fig. 402

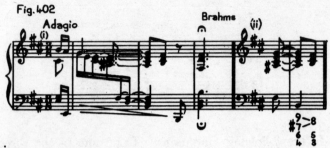

Exercises

1. Add alto and tenor parts.

Ex.1

2. Add three parts below, introducing double or single suspensions where appropriate.

3I. CHANGING NOTES: ACCENTED PASSING NOTES: PEDAL-POINTS: CHROMATIC DECORATION IN PART-WRITING

Changing Notes

1. We have already discussed and worked exercises on unaccented passing notes, auxiliary notes, additional harmony notes and anticipations (Chapters 13 and 22). Each of these is a form of decoration and can be used in conjunction with essential notes or with each other.

2. A changing note is also a means of decorating a phrase or a single note. It is an auxiliary—that is, an unessential note—which disregards, in part, the laws of movement as given in Chapter 13. This general definition will become more clear as we examine some of the principal patterns in which the changing note is included.

3. (*i*) An auxiliary, on moving (by step) from a harmony note, may leap backwards a third to another auxiliary provided the part then moves to a harmony note within that interval.

Fig. 403

4. The first and fourth semiquavers in each group in Fig. 403 are essential notes. The marked notes are unessential and, as they conform to the description above, are called changing notes. The following quotations from *Messiah* show this pattern in a sequence (Fig. 404) and in two parts (Fig. 405).

Fig. 404

5. The reverse of this pattern is also to be found.

Fig. 406

6. (*ii*) An auxiliary, having moved (by step) from an essential note may leap backwards to another essential note provided the interval is a third (see also para. 11). The leap may be upwards or downwards.

7. (*iii*) Rarely, a pattern of two consecutive changing notes (para. 3) resolve outside the interval they form. Care is needed in choosing the most suitable context.

8. (*iv*) There is in the music of the sixteenth and early seventeenth centuries a changing note pattern which is important to students of counterpoint. A part, in negotiating the interval of a fourth, steps downwards one degree and then leaps the remaining third to the new harmony note. This pattern, known as the *nota cambiata*, is illustrated in Fig. 411 (l). It is as if a step-wise passage employing two passing notes has been interrupted (m).

9. The following features of the *nota cambiata* pattern should be remembered. (*i*) The first note is a dotted unit of time (in this case a minim); (*ii*) it can be on any beat of the bar, but is most commonly sounded on a weak beat and tied over to a strong; (*iii*) the fourth note steps upward to the note omitted by the leap; (*iv*) while it is often used in cadences (Figs. 411 and 413) it also has its place elsewhere in a phrase.

10. The changing note in this pattern may clash with the logical movement of other parts (Fig. 414 (l)): this is accepted by the masters of the sixteenth century. More rarely the fourth note of the pattern does not follow its expected course (m).

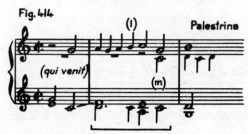

11. (*v*) Changing notes are to be found in other patterns. Since they are usually features of a period or composer they should be closely studied and only introduced into your own writing when stylistically appropriate. Thus, a modification of pattern (*ii*) may lead to a wider interval than that of a third.

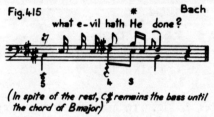

(Many composers have written passages in which a part leaps by a wider interval than a third from an essential to a non-harmony note; not infrequently the latter appears on analysis to be an appoggiatura. Some examples follow which you should compare with Figs. 403–414.)

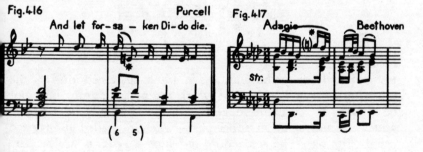

Fig. 418

Accented Passing Notes

12. The reference to unaccented passing notes in Book I implied that there might be another form of passing note. There is: it is the unessential note which is accented as it moves by step between two harmony notes.

Fig. 419

The marked notes in Fig. 419 are accented passing notes. It is true they are appoggiaturas, for so we would have termed them in Chapter 16. But not every appoggiatura is a passing note (compare Figs. 420 and 419). There is no need to labour this definition: 'accented passing note' is a term you will meet in your studies, and its nature and function are not hard to understand.

Fig. 420

Pedal-points

13. A pedal, or pedal-point, is a pitch sustained during the sounding of several chords of which the pedal may or may not be a part. As the name suggests, a pedal is usually in the bass; but it can also be in an upper part—when it is called an inverted pedal (Fig. 62). The restrictions to which a pedal is subject are: (*i*) it should be either the tonic or the dominant[1]; (*ii*) it must be an essential note of the chord on which the pedal-point begins;

---

[1] Pedals on other degrees are rare.

(*iii*) it must not move (that is, cease to be a pedal) until it again becomes a part of the prevailing harmony. A pedal may effectively be broken when it becomes the seventh of a dominant chord, such as $\frac{4}{2}$ (Fig. 423). Care should be taken in quitting a pedal on a six-four.

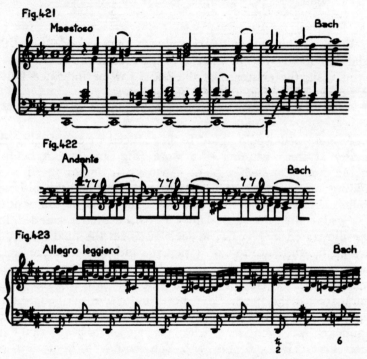

Fig. 421

Maestoso

Bach

Fig. 422

Andante

Bach

Fig. 423

Allegro leggiero

Bach

14. A pedal note need not sound continuously. It is sufficient that intermittent notes shall establish in the ear one predominant pitch (Figs. 422 and 423).

15. A pedal may be decorated—as by appoggiaturas or broken-chord patterns.

Fig. 424

Allegro

Beethoven

Fig. 425

16. When analysing and figuring chords above a pedal-point the pedal is ignored—except when it is the root of the chord above. If you wish, the existence of the pedal can be indicated below the figures. Thus, Fig. 422 will be figured

$$\text{I} \quad \text{IV} \quad \text{V}^6_5 \quad \text{I}$$

Tonic Ped. ————

17. A tonic pedal-point may be introduced in establishing the tonality at the beginning of a work (Fig. 421 and A below). On the dominant such a point can have an imposing effect in building up a climax and preparing the ear for the ultimate resolution on to the tonic. The continuation of a composition on a pedal after the tonic chord has been finally sounded has been illustrated in Fig. 62; in such instances the final resolution may be by the addition of a plagal cadence (as in the Lasso example quoted), though it is equally possible to conclude with a chord of the dominant or diminished seventh (on the super-tonic) against the pedal. The more impressive the pedal-point, the bigger and more expansive must be the composition in which it appears; yet even the briefest passage on a pedal can have great effect (Figs. 356 and 493). You should not hesitate to try your hand at using this device.

18. Examine the following works which contain pedal-points: note particularly the methods by which they are established and quitted.

    (A) Establishing the tonality:

        Bach, St. John Passion, No. 1.

        Bach, Mass in B minor, No. 15 (' Et incarnatus ').

        Handel, *Messiah*, No. 43 (' Thou shalt break them ').

        Haydn, ' London ' Symphony in D, 4th movement.

        Brahms, Requiem, 1st movement.

        Sibelius, Symphony No. 2 in D, 1st and 4th movements.

        (also Figs. 443, 445 and 485)

    (B) In the body of a composition:

        Bach, Christmas Oratorio, ' Pastoral Symphony,' No. 10.

Berlioz, Overture *Roman Carnival* (bars 300–344).

Sibelius, Symphony No. 2 in D, 4th Movement ('O'–12 after 'S').

Wagner, Prelude to *The Mastersingers* (bars 8–13; 31–33).

(also Fig. 530)

(C) Post-cadence Pedals:

Bach, Toccata (and Fugue) in D minor ('Dorian') for organ.

Bach, St. John Passion, No. 19 (last 3 bars).

Bach, Passacaglia for organ.

Brahms, Variations on a theme by Haydn, Op. 56.

Sibelius, Symphony No. 2 in D, 4th movement.

(also Figs. 522 and 523)

Longer sections with sustained pedal-points are to be found in:

Beethoven, Symphony No. 9 in D minor, Trio.

Brahms, Requiem, 3rd movement ($\frac{4}{2}$ — 'but the righteous souls').

Purcell, Fantasia on one note (for string quintet).

Schubert, 'The Erl King.'

Wagner, Prelude to *The Valkyrie*.

Walton, Symphony, 1st movement.

Exercises

1. Add a simple piano accompaniment below the following melodies. Name the instrument by which the melody is to be played, and add bow- or phrase-marks.

Chromatic Decoration

19. We have already used various forms of diatonic decoration; we turn now to those passing notes (accented and unaccented), auxiliary notes, and appoggiaturas which, being raised (or flattened) by accidentals, are chromatic decorations.

20. The introducton of chromatic decorations calls for care and discrimination. They can help to maintain the flow of a passage, or to produce an effect associated with a particular style. But if overdone they can make a composition sound frivolous, and possibly obscure the true harmonic progression.

21. Just as a chromatic chord can be introduced into a key without effecting or implying a modulation (Chapter 27), so a chromatic note used as a decoration does not, by itself, disturb the tonality. The difficulty facing a student in harmonizing a phrase which includes chromaticisms lies in distinguishing between essential accidentals and those which are only decorative.

Fig. 426

Fig. 427

Fig. 428

22. A chromatic passing note may lie between two essential notes a tone apart (Fig. 426 (l)), or be grouped with a diatonic passing note between essentials lying a third apart (m). They may be either unaccented or accented. Subject to the limitations outlined below, they may occur in rising or falling melodic phrases— though care is needed in the latter case, since chromatically flattened essential or diatonic passing notes can, on occasions, produce a trivial effect.

23. Chromatic passing notes are best used only in major keys; and even here there are restrictions on the choice of note to be altered chromatically. The fifth of I, IV, V, and V⁷ are suitable for this purpose; also the third of the first inversions of these chords. You should experiment at the piano and decide for yourself the context in which diatonic notes can satisfactorily be elaborated by chromatic passing notes.

24. Though such decorations must be used cautiously, they are of value when placed correctly—especially in maintaining the melodic flow or rhythm of a passage, and in helping to increase the interest or tension in a passage already presented in a simpler form. Fig. 429 (i) is stiff, both in its rhythm and its lack of melodic shape. By the addition of chromatic passing notes the same phrase flows more easily and gains in harmonic colour.

Fig. 429

25. Auxiliary notes were defined and discussed in Chapter 13. Reference was also made there (para. 10) to the possibility of an auxiliary moving only a semitone from the essential note from which it springs, should the diatonic interval of a whole tone be judged to be too wide. Such a reference was an anticipation of the present chapter. Chromatic auxiliaries may be either accented or unaccented. Like their diatonic equivalents, they may rise above or fall below the essential note from which they spring.

26. Appoggiaturas also have a chromatic form and require no explanation. A chromatic alteration may also be made to the ornamental resolution sometimes given to both appoggiaturas and suspensions—by which an interval of a third is reduced by a semitone (Fig. 431).

Fig. 430

Fig. 431

27. Reference must also be made to the Prelude to *Tristan*—a classic example of the expressive use of the appoggiatura in both its diatonic and chromatic forms. The opening bars are below. The key is A minor. At (l) the G♯ is a diatonic appoggiatura leaning towards the A which completes a chord of the French sixth; but at (m) the A♯ is a chromatic appoggiatura leaning to the B as part of V⁷. Again, at (n) the B is a diatonic appoggiatura (and once more the chord is the French sixth); while the C♯ at (o) is chromatic to V⁷ of C major.

Fig. 432

28. Look at the second subject of the finale (bar 71) of Mozart's symphony in G minor, K. 550. Here we find chromatic acciacaturas (l), a chromatically decorated resolution to a suspension (m), a chromatic appoggiatura (n), besides five chromatic passing notes. To anticipate what will be said in Chapter 32, the analysis of this passage (and hence the determining of the essential notes) is based on the assumption that there is only one harmony in each bar. (A helpful exercise is to copy out the essential harmonies of this passage and, afterwards, to add the chromatic decorations in a different coloured ink. Other passages of your choice should be treated similarly.)

Fig. 433

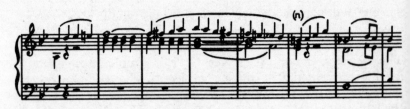

29. You will have noticed that the quotations on chromatic decoration are instrumental. Though the voice can (and is sometimes called on to) negotiate chromaticisms, this form of decoration is essentially unvocal; on the other hand, it is well suited to keyboard and other instrumental writing.

Exercises

2. Re-write the following, adding simple chromatic decoration.

3. Add simple accompaniments to the following melodies.

32. HARMONIC RHYTHM AND CHORD RECOGNITION

1. So long as the only unessential notes available to us were unaccented passing and auxiliary notes there was no difficulty in recognizing (on paper) any chord sounded or implied. Or, to put it differently, it was impossible (under these conditions) to mistake which were the essential notes when harmonizing a melody or a bass.

2. With the addition of appoggiaturas (and accented passing notes) more thought was needed both in the recognition of chords and in the harmonization of a given part. The situation will appear more hazardous still now that changing notes and chromatic decorations may be present to confuse us.

3. Some attention is given to chord recognition in this chapter. We must be able not only to identify the tonality underlying a passage, but also (and this is, perhaps, of greater importance) to choose the most suitable chords to support melodies.

4. Let us harmonize the following passage.

Fig. 434

But, you will object, these notes mean nothing as they stand: they have no time-values; and there is no time-signature. Correct; but you should also plead that there is no indication of the tempo at which they should be played—for tempo is an important factor in harmonization since it affects the number of harmonies in a bar. For instance, if these notes are arranged at a fairly slow pace in triple time, we are justified in sounding a fresh harmony on each beat:

Fig. 435

Andante (♩)

But when the tempo is increased until it becomes compound duple it would be fussy to have six harmonies in the bar—so we write only two chords for each half bar—one to cover the first two quavers, and one the third quaver:

Fig. 436

Allegretto (♩.)

The reduction in the number of chords (compared with Fig. 435) satisfies the ear by allowing the passage to flow more freely. But in making the alteration we find we are introducing three unessential notes: a changing note (l); an unaccented passing note (m); and an appoggiatura (n)—for the basic chord is II⁷ in D major. With a further increase in speed, this melody can be stripped still further of harmonies: two in the first bar and three in the second are sufficient.

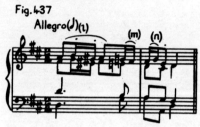

Fig. 437

There are several points to note in Fig. 437. We have introduced changing notes at (l) and (n), one pair of which has been altered chromatically; and at (m) there is an anticipation. Secondly, the *melodic* and *harmonic* rhythms are different, yet complementary, to one another. Compare the rhythmic outlines of these three versions:

Fig. 438

5. If we are asked to extend this passage we must maintain a suitable harmonic rhythm while at the same time making play with the chief characteristics of the original melody. Something on these lines might result:

Fig. 439

You will see that, as in Fig. 437, the harmonic rhythm is not constant. It beats faster at the cadences. The same principle is at work in the well-known theme from Haydn's ' Surprise ' symphony. Here there are six regular harmonic beats (one in each bar) before the pulse is doubled at the half-close; thereafter the harmonic rhythm becomes more flexible and never reverts to the original.

Fig. 440

6. Harmonic rhythm refers (*i*) to the frequency of harmony changes and (*ii*) to the rhythm by which those harmonies are presented. But there may also be an underlying rhythm which supplements that of the melody and harmony. Look at the quotation below from Brahms. Basically there are two harmonies in a bar; but behind the broad sweep of the melody and harmony there is a third (a quaver) pattern which is phrased within itself by rhythmic ' cadences.'

Fig.441

7. An underlying rhythm is to be found in many of the songs of Schubert and Brahms, to name no others. In Schubert's ' Wohin? ' (' Whither? ') the right hand of the accompaniment is engaged in rustling semiquavers from start to finish. Yet the harmonic rhythm of the (first verse of the) melody is both slow moving and of the simplest kind.

Fig. 443

The moral may well be that the greater the number of notes and the faster they are played, the simpler should be the harmonic progression.

8. Sustained notes are an opportunity for harmonic and rhythmic invention rather than a signal for hesitation in all parts. We know that if a sustained note falls by step we may be able to introduce a suspension. Here is a quotation from Bach in which three such opportunities arise. In the first bar there is but one harmony to each beat (compare Fig. 436), though a gentle lilt is maintained by the repetition of the bass note (at an octave distance); the second bar expands into two harmonies per beat.

Fig. 444

9. Again, in the final movement of his 'Requiem' Brahms supports a sustained melody with four harmonies in each bar, but adds greatly to the total effect by dividing each crotchet into throbbing quavers. Test the difference this underlying rhythm makes by playing the accompaniment as a succession of crotchets, and then repeating the passage as written.

Fig. 445

10. The foregoing paragraphs show that (*i*) the number of harmonies in a bar is largely dependent on the tempo and character of the composition; (*ii*) the changing harmonies form a rhythmic pattern which will support, but not necessarily coincide with, the phrasing and rhythm of the melody; and (*iii*) additional, independent rhythms may be superimposed on those of the melody and harmony. These factors must be uppermost in the mind of a composer; we shall refer to them again in the chapters which follow. Meanwhile you should keep your ear and eye open for the harmonic rhythm in the music you are hearing or performing; learn as much as you can from your personal experience.

11. Returning to the question of chord recognition, let us add a simple accompaniment to this melody.

Fig. 446

Bars 2 and 4 clearly demand two harmonies each (ignoring any movement from $\frac{5}{3}$ to $\frac{6}{3}$ of the same chord). How many in bar 1? Is a chord of A major sufficient or suitable by itself? If you try it you will probably find it colourless—especially as the first chord of bar 2 must also be A major. Can bar 1 be accompanied by I–V? Yes, if the E and B are interpreted as essential notes.

What of bar 3? Will I–IV be suitable? Possibly; but it will result in the unenterprising harmonic rhythm of

I V I V I IV V I

and emphasize the tonic yet a third time. Bar 3 can also be accompanied by VI–I–IV–II, which will break up the harmonic rhythm into

I V I V VI I IV II V+3 I

This is an improvement. The underlying rhythm of the accompaniment must also be considered. At its simplest it can follow that of the harmony, yet there will be greater interest if the semiquaver figure of the melody is introduced into the accompaniment in bars 2 and 4. Here is a possible solution, with the various rhythms tabulated below:

Fig. 447

Fig. 448

Rhythms:—
melody
accompaniment
harmony

Fig. 449

Allegretto

12. At Fig. 449 is a melody which, at first sight, seems to demand a more complex harmonization. Do bars 1 and 3 carry four harmonies each? If so, what are they? If you are not satisfied with your experiments at the piano, try regarding the first semiquaver in both these bars as an appoggiatura; now what do we find? I—V^7 for bar 1; V^7–I^9 for bar 3. The remainder is straightforward—though you should note the movement in the accompaniment while the solo part is sustained.

Fig. 450

13. By examining the function of the individual notes of a melody it is possible to choose a suitable harmonic support. Essential notes are perfectly clear in broken-chord patterns: the difficulties arise when they are masked by passing notes and auxiliaries. Our choice of harmonies is also guided by the need to establish the tonic and then to move away from it—as in Fig. 447, and as we discussed in Chapter 18. And, lastly, the number and rhythm of the harmonies in the bar must be taken into account. All these factors contribute to the musical harmonization of a given passage.

Fig. 451

14. Unexpected progressions may need special study. How will you harmonize Fig. 451? In particular, what is the role of the marked notes? Changing notes? Appoggiaturas? Try adding an accompaniment at the piano. Have you noticed that each

marked note has been sounded two quavers earlier (presumably as an essential note)? Does not this suggest that the passage contains the elaboration of several 7–6 suspensions? Fig. 452 gives the harmonic outline: what Bach wrote is at Fig. 453.

Fig. 452

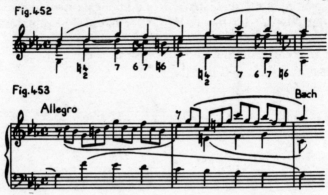

Fig. 453

Exercises

Below the following:

1. Pencil in the chords implied by the melodic line.
2. Sketch the probable harmonic progression of an accompaniment for piano.
3. Add simple decorations which will give character to the accompaniment and provide a rhythmic pattern complementary to that of the melody.

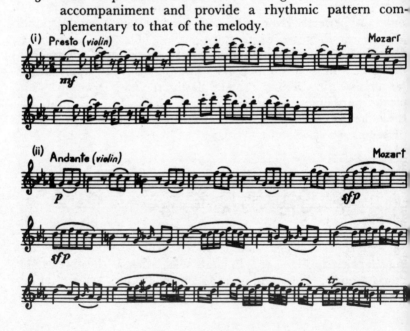

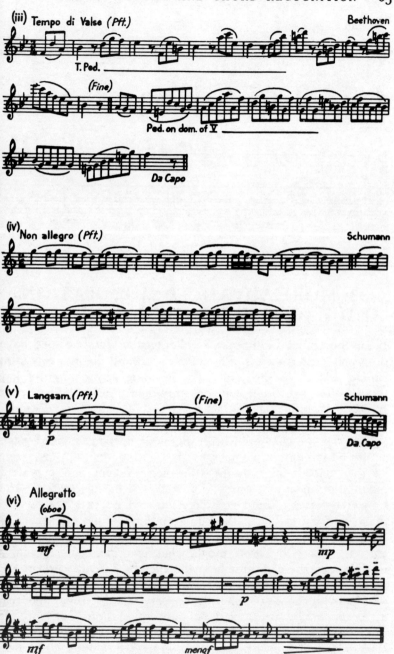

33. MORE ADVANCED MODULATION AND HARMONIZATION IN FOUR PARTS

1. In the course of the earlier chapters of this book we have discussed various means of modulating beyond the five keys most closely related to the tonic. To negotiate any change of key requires thought. Shall it be accomplished in a gradual manner (possibly by using chords common to both keys), or does the context demand a more sudden effect? What is the most suitable ' route ' for the change? And is there one particular chord (such as the Neapolitan or augmented sixth) which can appropriately be the central point of the transition? Fluent and confident modulation in any direction is an essential in composition. The subject deserves careful consideration and practice. Sit at the piano and try to ' feel,' through your fingers, the movement of the tonality to this or that new key. The eye (until it is experienced) cannot by itself judge what comprises a satisfactory modulation; the ear must help the eye. By careful work at the piano you can cultivate an instinct for key changes; and you will learn to choose the chords necessary to bring them about.

2. In the first instance, a series of four or five chords outlining the modulation is sufficient. The passage should then be repeated with the addition of a few unessential notes to give colour and interest. (When putting the result down on paper add phrase-marks—

for no passage, however short, should be shapeless, and the shape which is in your mind must be communicated to those who are to see or play your work.) Compare the two versions of each of these examples:

Fig. 454

Fig. 455

3. Modulations may both begin and end on either a root position or first inversion. In the following exercises it is assumed that the opening key has already been established.

Exercises

1. Modulate in a few chords
   (*i*) from C major to each of the following keys:
         G, Ab, E major and e, d and f minor.
   (*ii*) from d minor to: Bb, A, F major and g and a minor.
   (*iii*) from A to C; G to Eb; D to b; c to Eb; e to B.
2. Add simple decorations to each of the modulations in Exercise 1. Write for four voices, or string quartet, or for soprano voice with a three-part piano accompaniment. Add phrase- or bowing-marks.
3. You may find it helpful at this point to tabulate all the keys to which you have learned to move from (say) C major and minor; you will find you have the necessary information (in Chapters 18–29) to modulate to some ten major and the same number of minor keys. But, of these, some will be remote from the original key and, on this account, will only rarely be your goal. In Chapter 18 our modulations were made only to those

keys most closely related to the tonic; though you now have more freedom of choice, the selection of keys to which you are most likely to be asked to modulate are contained in the figure below.

Fig. 456

5. On the diagram of the cycle of keys (Fig. 58) all these lie near the original tonic. So from any given major key you should be prepared to modulate to the major of II, III, ♭III, IV, V, VI, ♭VI, ♭VII and the minor of II, III, IV, V, and VI; and from any minor key to the major of its ♭III, V, ♭VI, ♭VII and the minor of its IV and V.

6. Though the exercises in this chapter will be short and compact, it is possible for them to be artistic compositions in miniature if you make good use of any features which present themselves. These features—simple rhythmic, melodic or (to a lesser extent) harmonic patterns—will provide material for imitation, and thus contribute to the unity of the composition. In Fig. 454 (*ii*) the rising quavers in the soprano and bass are imitated elsewhere, so that this melodic shape becomes a recognizable feature. In Fig. 455 there is a rhythmic pattern which is passed through all parts in turn.

Exercises

3. Begin as follows and modulate in a few bars to each of the keys named. Add phrase- or bowing-marks.

to D, e, E♭, F, g, A, a, and B♭

(ii) (Ob. and Pft.)

to f, G, ab, Bb, Cb, and c

(iii) (Str.)

to c#, Db, d#, E, f#, Gb, g# and A

(iv) (Str.)

to D, e, G, A and f#

(v) (Vln. and Pft.)

to Ab, bb, C, Db and Eb

. Re-write your modulations in Exercise 1, introducing melodic or rhythmic patterns of your own invention.

. When presented with a succession of keys through which to modulate, any principal cadences should, if possible, be in keys most closely related to the original tonic. In a short exercise one such cadence will usually suffice, and the dominant or the relative minor (or major) are obvious choices of key. Other changes in tonality can be established at less prominent cadences or treated as transient modulations. In this connection it is not always convenient or necessary to sound the new tonic in root position; the first inversion is often more suitable; and the

dominant seventh alone may prove sufficient to fix the modulation
in the mind before moving to yet another key.

Fig.457

8. Sequences are effective in passages involving modulation
especially if the two keys lie a tone or a semitone apart. Th
sequence quoted from Mozart (Fig. 458) is exact; but ther

is no merit in a note for note reproduction if the result is empty. It is often better to vary the harmonization of a melodic sequence, especially if a second reproduction is demanded—that is, the sounding of the same passage three times (Fig. 459).

Fig. 458

Allegretto

Mozart

Fig. 459

Andante

9. Modulations in the course of free composition will not normally succeed one another so rapidly or in so confined a space as in the exercises in this chapter. It is in the selection and placing of the cadences, and (by the use of rhythmic and melodic imitation) in the texture that the advanced quality of the harmonization chiefly lies—though modulation makes an important contribution to tonal balance. These factors contribute to style in music. For the purposes of this Course the style of writing is greatly influenced by the exercises set for you to work; but you should by now be trying your hand at original composition in which the style and content can (and, ideally, should) spring from your own imagination. It has already been said that you are a composer as soon as you write down the simplest musical passage: your claims to that title are greater still if the music springs wholly from your own head. But music writing is not a natural process, and much practice is needed to attain fluency; you will possibly never find it as easy to harmonize a melody as to write a letter or tot up a column of figures, yet many of the difficulties in expressing oneself in music can be reduced by steady practice in setting down your ideas on paper. And remem-

ber, freedom and originality do not mean release from the rules and customs of musical behaviour; on the contrary, just as you accept a code of behaviour in your daily life, so you should accept the musical code which has been outlined in this short Course.

10. In the exercises which conclude this chapter the melodic and rhythmic data should be continued and developed so as to create a complete and satisfactory whole. The modulations, though artificial, are intended as practice in the main subject of this chapter.

Exercises

5. Begin as given and, modulating as directed, write a movement of about sixteen bars. Write in either short or open score.

Ex. 5

(iv) Poco adagio

(Str.) p

through F, e, a, g to d

(v) Allegro

(Str.) mf

through g, b, f, Eb

34. MORE ADVANCED CONTRAPUNTAL WRITING IN TWO AND THREE PARTS

1. If you have worked through this Course thus far, perhaps you already own or have access to Thomas Morley's two- and three-part canzonets, and Bach's inventions in two and three parts. These volumes contain a rich store of information on the style and standard of contrapuntal writing to which you can very well set your hand at this stage. There are many other compositions which you can imitate if you will; but the collections mentioned are outstanding. Sing the canzonets; play the inventions; analyse all of them; compose pieces of a similar nature.

2. To be more advanced in contrapuntal writing is not to pack more harmonies into each bar, to use more complex chords, or to modulate more often and more remotely. Examination of the works referred to above will show you that this is not so. Rather is it the building of your composition on a well-balanced pattern in which quite simple material is presented clearly in accordance with a satisfactory key-plan. Composing such movements is not unlike writing a melody: there are many possible patterns, but the one chosen is delineated by cadences in chosen keys, by the presentation of contrasting material, and so on.

3. Look at Morley's two-part canzonet, ' Lo here another love.' This is built on three themes, the third being also presented in its inversion.

Fig. 460

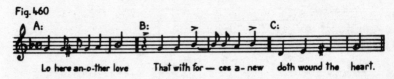

Lo here an-o-ther love   That with for — ces a-new   doth wound the   heart.

Both voices carry theme A in turn for four bars, then combine for a cadence in gV at bars 6/7, followed by another in gI at bars 8/9. These nine bars are then repeated with the voices changing parts.

Fig. 461

Morley

Theme B is heard only once in each voice, beginning in G minor and coming to gV five bars later at 22/23. Theme C next enters in G minor and the voices modulate to B flat before returning to the tonic and so to the final cadence. These sixteen bars are then repeated, the parts being reversed once more.

Fig. 462

4. It will be noticed that reference to the prevailing theme ceases at the onset of the cadence to that section. The form of this canzonet can therefore be outlined as:

||: A — cadence :||: B — cadence — C — cadence:||

Other canzonets have different shapes. The words have an influence on the form, for the number of themes is dependent on the number of ideas springing from the verse. (See also Fig. 167.)

5. Morley's three-part canzonets are similar in character to those in two parts. The thematic material is presented by imitative entries, and each subject is discarded as the composition moves

on to fresh words; though in many instances the imitation is
not continued so strictly or for so many measures as in the duos.

Fig. 463

6. Before working the exercises given at the end of the chapter
you should analyse the harmonic progression of some examples
from both Morley's collections. It will be seen that they lend
support to the principle outlined in Chapter 32, para. 5.

7. The greater freedom in Bach's inventions arises from the
absence of words to govern the music, and from the changed
outlook on musical style. The madrigalian custom of discarding
material once the applicable words have been sung has given
way to a more constant repetition, and return, of the chief
themes. The first invention in two parts is built on one subject
only; in the twenty-two bars this is stated thirty-seven times—
nineteen of them in the inversion. But still the form is clearly
mapped out. At the end of bar 2 the tonic is re-emphasized
before the parts move more freely and lead to the dominant at
the end of bar 6. The music then passes through D minor and
so to a cadence in A minor, the relative minor of the tonic

(bar 14). During the remaining eight bars CV is once more established, and CIV is touched on before the final cadence in the tonic (see Chapter 18, paras. 24-26). Quite apart from the ingenious use of the original subject, the form and the key-plan of this invention are perfectly clear.

Fig. 465

8. The two-part invention in D minor has a different construction.   A two-bar semiquaver pattern with the striking characteristic of a leap of a diminished seventh is the principal subject; and against it the second part begins by sounding broken chords in quavers before moving with greater independence.

Fig. 466

Here again the key-plan is clearly set out. First there is the re-emphasis of D minor at bar 5, and then the expansion of the music until a modulation leads to the first chief cadence in F major. Moving through G minor to the dominant of A minor, the next cadence is in aI, after which a quick succession of modulations to G minor, F major and D minor prepares for the final cadence after an interruption at bar 49. Once more we see how a single thematic idea (presented in this instance twenty-one times) can build up a satisfactory composition by working within a carefully constructed key-plan. You will find it helpful to write out the implied tonality of each bar of this invention as a simple chord, or as a bass with figures.

9. Reference was made in Chapter 12, para. 16, to the answer of a tonic entry by one in the dominant, and vice versa. It is usual also for the dominant and tonic *notes* at the beginning of a

subject to be answered by the tonic and dominant *notes* of the next entry—in spite of the changed interval involved.

Fig. 467

Thus, in Fig. 467 (*i*), though the first entry in G is answered by one in D, the first *note* of the answer is G, and not A. This is called a tonal answer. In (*ii*) the same applies, but here the note at (m) must be a third above that preceding it in order to obtain the correct tonality in the answer (which is in A♯ minor). A tonal answer frequently requires an alteration of interval in this manner. In the example at (*iii*), the answer (o) demands a step of only a semitone, and not an interval of a third as at (n).

10. While recommending Morley's canzonets and Bach's inventions as patterns for imitation, there is no need to copy them exactly or to write at such length in the first instance. The essentials are for the result to be well-balanced and musicianly. Look at the following passage for two voices.

Fig. 468

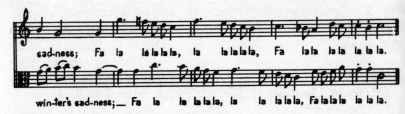

sad-ness;   Fa la   la la la la,   la   la la la la,   Fa   la la   la la   la la la.

win-ter's sad-ness;— Fa la   la la la la, la   la   la la la, Fa la la la   la la la.

In this miniature canzonet both parts begin with a leap of a
fourth. (This is a real answer since the interval sounded by the
second voice corresponds to that in the subject.) Each voice
has the subject once before the passage moves to the dominant
at bar 5. The fa las are sung to a modified version of the subject.
In the penultimate bar, CIV is touched before the final cadence.
You will see that the imitation is not always exact. Analyse the
implied chords; study the harmonic progression; and examine
the treatment of all tied notes.

11. Now turn to the following passage for three stringed instruments.

Fig. 469

The first two entries of the two-bar subject are (as we might
expect) in the tonic and dominant, followed by a third entry

in the tonic. Together, the parts move to the relative major—
without reference to the subject, yet in character with it. At bar 9
the cadence in the relative major is made the beginning of a fresh
set of entries—F major, the dominant of B flat, and one in B flat
itself which maintains the rhythm of the subject while altering
the melodic interval. In bar 12, FIV is treated as dVI; and so
the tonality returns to the tonic. Note that whereas the subject
enters only thrice in bars 1-4, it is presented five times in bars
9-13. Again, analyse the chords; study the harmonic progression; and examine the treatment of all tied notes.

Exercises

1. Add a second part to the following.

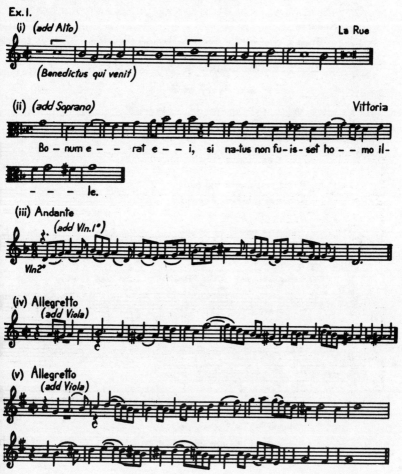

(vi) Allegro
(add Violin)

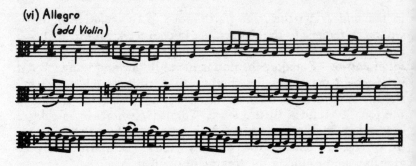

2. Write simple canzonets on the following material.

Ex.2

(i) Andante

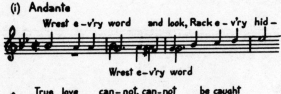

Wrest every word and look,
Rack every hidden thought,
Or fish with golden hook;
True love cannot be caught.

(Campion)

(ii) Allegro

Welcome to this flowery place,
Fair Goddess and sole Queen of grace.

(Campion)

(iii) Allegro

Come a-shore,_____ come, come, mer-ry mates, come, come

Come a - shore,   come,   come, mer-ry mates

Sum-mon e-v'ry man,   Sum-mon e-v'ry man

pates: Sum-mon e-v'ry man   his knight,

Come ashore, come, merry mates,
With your nimble heels and pates:
Summon every man his knight,
Enough honoured is this night.

(Campion)

(iv) Allegretto

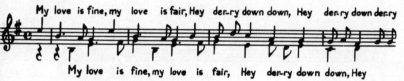

My love is fine, my love is fair, Hey der-ry down down, Hey   der-ry down der-ry

My love   is fine, my love is fair, Hey der-ry down down, Hey

My love is fine, my love is fair,
Hey derry down, down derry,
No maid with her may well compare
In Kent or Canterbury.
Hey derry down, down derry.

(Deloney)

3. Complete the following.

Ex.3
(i)

Weelkes

Say   wanton will you love me? I love no long de-

Say_____ wanton will you   love__ me?   I

Say   wanton will   .you   love__ me?   I

-lay-ing, no long de - lay - ing   I love no long de - lay - ing, de-lay - ing

(ii)   Woelkes

(Clear wells spring not   cheer-ful-ly)

(Sweet birds sing not   cheer-ful-ly)

(Loud   bells ring not cheerfully)

(iii)   Tomkins

love ___ cease tor-ment - - - - - ing, (etc.)

love ___ cease tor - - ment- ing (etc.)

love cease   tor - ment - ing,   tor - - ment-

4. Write two-part inventions for harpsichord or piano on the
   following material. The principal phrases are marked.

Ex.4

(i) Allegro moderato

5. Complete the following for string trio or organ.

Ex.5

(ii) Allegro

(iii) Moderato

(iv) Allegretto

35. HARMONIZATION OF CHORALES IN THE STYLE OF J. S. BACH

1. The very large number of harmonizations of chorales left us by Bach demonstrates clearly his views on the structure of harmony founded on contrapuntal principles. A close familiarity with this collection will provide you with a sound knowledge of the greater part of harmony used throughout the eighteenth and nineteenth centuries. A copy of one of the several editions containing all Bach's chorale settings should find its way on to your shelves without delay if you are intending to study music seriously.

2. The German chorale does not move fast; though in its dignified gait it should never be allowed to drag. There is no parallel with the lightness and gaiety of many English hymn-tunes. According to the character of the particular melody, the tempo of a German chorale in Common time may vary between 40 and 60 crotchets to the minute.

3. Every word is sung by each voice. Though one part may anticipate a syllable or delay it, the words are (in general) sung

together by all voices. A slur in the melody indicates that the harmonization may be either by a single chord or by a number of notes slurred similarly.

Fig. 4.70

4. Some of Bach's settings of these chorales are almost continuously note for note; a small number (such as one harmonization of 'Jesu meine Freude'[1]) are clothed with such a degree of elaboration as to pass beyond the limits of what we may regard, in this chapter, as the accepted chorale style. But the style of the large majority is simple, while allowing considerable freedom in the part-writing. These are the models you should study and try to imitate. As you look at these chorales you will appreciate that Bach's aim was to preserve the interest and flow of the individual parts as they support the melody; and as you play them on the piano you will come to feel that the intermittent quaver-movement is a marked feature in sustaining the rhythm of the phrases. In this style the parts cross when necessary, and the range of the voices (especially the tenor and bass) is sometimes wider than we have met so far.

Fig. 4.71

[1] The fourth verse (seventh movement) of the motet of this name.

Fig. 472

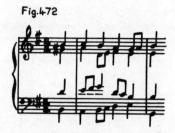

In preserving the sweeping contours of the voices under the chorale, Bach employs many accented, as well as unaccented, passing notes, and accepts striking dissonances (usually on unaccented beats) brought about by the logical progression of the separate parts.

Fig. 473

Fig. 474

(Refer also to Fig. 287 which was quoted in discussing anticipations.)

5. Suspensions play an important part in these settings, yet appoggiaturas are almost totally excluded. The preparation of suspensions may be a full beat, as is customary; but whenever the circumstances demand it, Bach reduces this to a half-beat.

Fig. 475

6. The bass in these chorales will on occasion rise above the tenor and so produce a $^6_4$ in a surprising context, or some other dissonance. In Bach's time, chorales were accompanied by organ or orchestra (or both), so that the vocal bass would be

re-inforced an octave lower (by the pedals or string bass), thus correcting the position of the offending chord (Fig. 476). To avoid confusion, the bass in your own work should be in the octave which will produce the chord intended.

Fig. 476

7. While most of the cadences do no more than terminate a phrase in a simple and direct manner, some final cadences are embellished by additional chords and so have a richness and beauty reminiscent of the polyphonic closes of the sixteenth century (Figs. 521–523). Such instances in Bach merit a study of the harmonies involved; most are inverted pedals, the underlying parts maintaining the movement and character of the preceding bars.

Fig. 477

Fig. 478

Fig. 479

Bach rarely introduces a suspension or appoggiatura on the final chord of a phrase. You should follow his example on this point.

8. The fall of the leading note to the dominant in final (and other principal) cadences is a common feature in Bach's settings; he preferred the final chord to be complete with both third and fifth (Figs. 470, 475, 482). To achieve this it is sometimes necessary for the leading note to move to the mediant. Thus:

Fig. 480

9. Before working exercises in imitation of Bach's chorales you should revise Chapter 17, paras. 17-19 (passing six-fours in approaching a cadence), and Chapter 21, para. 14 (the super-tonic seventh as found in Bach's works).

10. Bach wrote very few chorale melodies himself. Some he set were inherited from an earlier century and are modal in structure. He did not harmonize these in a strictly modal style. (This aspect of chorale settings is beyond the scope of this Course and can be studied later). But just as he felt free to choose the harmonies best suited to the purpose in hand, so Bach felt himself at liberty to decorate the melodies. Here are three versions of the same line:

Fig. 481

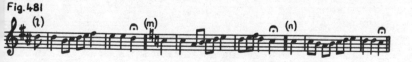

11. One complete example from Bach is given below as a pattern for your own work. Other chorales harmonized by him are to be found in many English hymn books: ' Nun danket,' ' Ein' feste Burg,' ' Nun ruhen alle Wälder ' (sometimes called ' Innsbruck ') are well-known. In studying Fig. 482, notice that the tonic is established in the first phrase, before the harmony moves to a half-close at the second cadence; and that the relative minor is touched at the opening of the third phrase, though it surrenders at once to the dominant of G major. If you play this tune over you will find that the chromatic chord of F♯ major (in bar 3) does not disturb the tonality of GV. When planning the harmonization of a chorale, begin by deciding the tonality of the cadence-points (Chapter 18); be sure to establish your tonic before moving elsewhere, and to re-establish it in the last line. Bach varied his harmonies in different settings of the same tune. You should do the same. It is valuable practice to extemporize several harmonies of the same phrase at the piano. Copy Bach's style closely, and absorb all you can of the spirit of his chorale harmonizations.

Fig. 482

Exercises
1. Analyse the chords in all the quotations given in this chapter.
2. Harmonize the following chorales in the style of J. S. Bach.

Ex.2

(vii)

(viii)

3. Harmonize these chorale phrases in two different ways in the style of J. S. Bach.

Ex.3

4. Transpose the quotations in this chapter into named keys at the piano.

APPENDIX 'C'
Writing for Strings

1. By ' strings' we may mean several stringed instruments to each part playing in a group (as in an orchestra); a chamber-music ensemble in which there is only one player to a part (as in a string quartet, trio, sextet, and so on); or (in this context) a solo stringed instrument accompanied by some other instrument or group of instruments (as in a sonata or a concerto). But before reading these paragraphs, revise Chapter 9, paras. 5-30, in which the essence of *vocal* writing is set down.

2. Compared with voices, strings have a much wider range (Fig. 483) and a greater melodic flexibility (Fig. 90). Thus, though voice parts can effectively be reproduced on strings, the true character of string writing does not emerge until some of the restrictions on the voice are brushed aside. But the laws of part-writing remain unchanged.

Fig. 483

3. According to the requirements of the composition, string writing can embody these features:

    (*i*)   Wide leaps (Fig. 484).
    (*ii*) Wide spacing between the parts (Figs. 99, 107).

   (iii)   Plentiful use of rests (Figs. 377, 406, 444).
   (iv)   Independence of movement and rhythm between parts
           (Figs. 356, 441).
   (v)   Rhythmic patterns which may be more immediately striking
           than the melodic line (Figs. 290, 485).

Fig. 484

Allegro   Beethoven

Fig. 485

Allegro   Schubert

4. The following should always be added to the score of a work for
strings (and, where applicable, to all instrumental and keyboard
writing). See also Appendix B.
   (vi)   Bowing- or phrase-marks. (If there are no bow-marks the
           string player will give each note a fresh bow.)
   (vii)   Interpretation- and accent-marks (Fig. 486).
   (viii) Directions as to volume (*p*, *mf*, *ff*, etc.).

Fig. 486

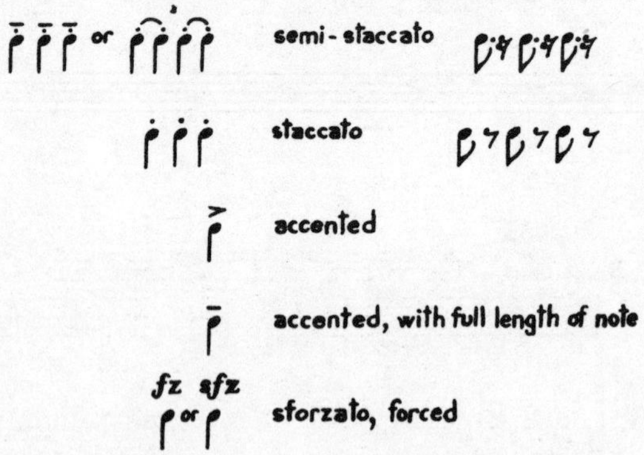

semi-staccato

staccato

accented

accented, with full length of note

fz sfz
sforzato, forced

5. It is impossible in this Course to explain how to write for strings.
You should help yourself by keeping your eyes open for examples of
the principal styles of string writing, and by listening carefully to the

effect and quality of tone produced by the massed strings of an orchestra and the solo units of a chamber-music ensemble. Build up your own library of scores illustrating the various styles of string writing. For this purpose the following might be a beginning: Purcell's *Chacony* in G minor; Bach's 3rd and 5th Brandenburg concertos; a concerto grosso by Handel; Haydn's string quartets op. 64 No. 5 in D (the 'Lark'), op. 3 No. 5 in F, and op. 33 No. 2 in E flat; Mozart's string quartets in D minor, K. 421, in B flat, K. 458 (the 'Hunt'), and in C, K. 465; Beethoven's string quartets op. 18 No. 1 in F, and op. 59 No. 2 in E minor; Elgar's Serenade in E minor for Strings, and the Introduction and Allegro; Vaughan Williams's Fantasia on a theme by Thomas Tallis; besides the scores of some classical symphonies.

6. It is difficult to define and describe the principal string styles. The following may be taken as a rough guide:

A. Quasi-Vocal (Early Seventeenth Century): not far removed from the madrigal of the sixteenth century. Imitation may guide the movement of the parts, for each has its own individuality.

B. Late Seventeenth Century: The example by Purcell at Fig. 176 is the opening of a simple yet very beautiful dance for strings. At Fig. 489 is a hornpipe in which all four parts have a freedom bounded only by the need to present the harmonies clearly. (You should assume that double-basses are doubling the cello part an octave lower in all quotations for orchestra.)

Fig. 489 Allegretto Purcell

Vln. 1
Vln. 2
Vla.
Vc. & Db

C. Bach and Handel: In a fragment from a slow movement by Bach, quoted at Fig. 444, a melody in the top part is supported by detached chords before the whole ensemble combines for the cadence. In a similar manner, at Fig. 490, two principal parts alternate, with a light accompaniment underneath (which would include a continuo). Note that the bass takes up the dotted rhythm when it ceases in the violins.

Fig. 490 Bach

There are many vigorous allegro movements in Bach's orchestral suites and Brandenburg concertos, and in the concerti grossi and operatic overtures of Handel; all these works contain fugal writing which is worthy of study. But for your immediate needs, this fragment from Handel illustrates his treatment of a more harmonic texture.

Fig. 491

D. Haydn and Mozart: It was in this period that the string quartet reached so high a degree of perfection. Here we find, at times, the support of a melody by parts which, though subordinate, have their own individuality; and, at others, a more equal status between the four instruments (Fig. 496). In either style, the harmonic foundation is always clear; each part contributes to this clarity and does not move in a haphazard fashion. In writing your exercises in recent chapters you have tried to give life to the voice parts by adding simple decorations. In analysing the string writing of the classics you should reverse the process; strip away the complexities (in your mind) so as to lay bare the harmonies underneath. For instance, you are familiar with such a sequence of chords as this:

Fig. 492

These chords are the foundation of a passage from one of Haydn's quartets. By passing notes and auxiliaries, by rests and sustained chords he embellishes this simple outline as follows:

Fig. 493

Play the three lower parts without the first violin. You will find they present a rhythm which is complementary to that of the melody. Notice, too, the similarities and differences between the pulse of the two halves of the accompaniment.

Fig. 494

Fig. 493 represents string writing at its best. There is independence, variety and above all clarity of purpose. It does not lie comfortably for the piano—but this is one of the signs of a good quartet style.

One more quotation from Haydn (Fig. 495) to illustrate the variety of his rhythm and texture. The pattern of the accompaniment to bars 1-3 is simple and adds a sense of urgency to the melody; yet before we can tire of it a fresh pulse closes the phrase at bar 4. Rests are a feature in bars 5 and 6, before four neat chords introduce the only moment of legato playing in the whole passage. In looking at this quotation you should ask yourself, ' how would I have harmonized the first violin part in bars 5 and 6? How would I have dealt with the rests? '

Fig. 495

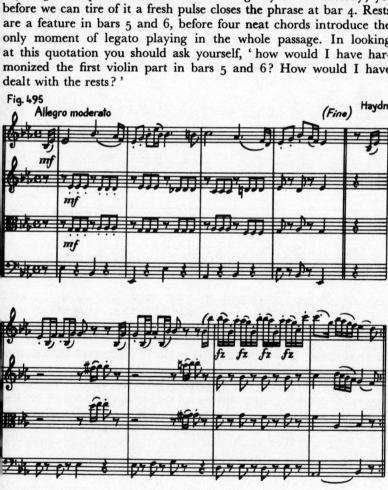

In a short extract from Mozart the four instruments have a greater
equality than the last two examples. The unity which results does
nothing to restrict the freedom of each part. Look at the contour of
the viola in bars 5–7. Examine the repetition of the cadence in the last
bar. Analyse the chords in the whole of this passage and note the
harmonic progression.

Fig. 496

7. From these quotations you will begin to understand that writing
for strings entails much more than changing the tone-colour from tha'
of voices or the piano. String writing adds life and interest to the
expression of quite simply constructed music; and it tests the compose
in his ability to control texture as well as harmony and counterpoint
8. If the music demands a more obviously harmonic texture—tha
is, without devices of imitation or independent movement—the chor
progression can be presented in the form of a rhythmic or melodi
figure. But the warning must be added that no figure should b
maintained too long without variation. Haydn (Fig. 495) allows th

figure of repeated chords to be heard for no more than three bars before abandoning it. Do not regard a simple chord-figure as an easy way of jotting down an accompaniment without thought or invention. The figure must suit the context, and never outstay its welcome. In particular, the use of *tremolando* chords should be avoided except for brief moments of special significance. Some examples of chordal figurations effective in string writing are given below.[1] Others are at Figs. 96, 233, 280, 356, 406, 433 and 444.

Fig.497

[1] These should not be applied to styles of music before 1750.

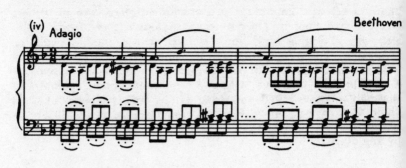

APPENDIX 'D'
Writing for the Pianoforte

1. The piano has long been the musician's maid-of-all-work. So often is it called on to represent unpianistic resources—at this moment a choir, at the next an orchestra—that a reminder is necessary from time to time that it has many styles of its own which cannot be reproduced by any other means.

2. Since it is reasonably simple to buy or borrow piano music of every period and description, it will be sufficient to tabulate the principal styles and refer to one or two representative works of each. Though true piano music did not appear until after 1750, it is unwise to ignore keyboard music of an earlier age which, written originally for the virginal, harpsichord, or clavichord, is habitually played on the piano today.

A. Virginal music of the Tudor period. While much of the writing is reminiscent of consort music for viols (such as fantasias and dance movements) or madrigals of the time, a style more suited to keyboard playing was being developed in preludes, grounds and variations on song tunes. But with the exception of scalic passages, the influence of vocal writing is still so marked that the progression of the parts can usually be traced. See the works of John Bull; Orlando Gibbons; William Byrd (Variations on ' O Mistris Myne ', ' Sellinger's Rownde ', The Bells, Suite: ' The Battell ', Pavan and Galliard: ' The Earle of Salisbury ').

Fig.498

Byrd

Fig. 499

B. Bach, Handel, Couperin, and the early eighteenth-century composers writing for harpsichord or clavichord. A contrapuntal texture in two, three, or more parts (inventions, suites, fugues) (Figs. 465 and 466). Also a more homophonic style, often decked out with cadenza passages (as in preludes and toccatas), but still influenced in the part-writing by contrapuntal considerations (Figs. 422 and 423). See Bach's inventions, French and English suites, partitas, the Anna Magdalena Book, the 'Well-tempered Clavier' (the '48'); Handel's suites for harpsichord; Couperin's 'Ordres'.

Fig. 500

C. The so-called classical period of Mozart, Haydn, and Beethoven —not forgetting less well-known keyboard composers such as C. P. E. Bach, Clementi, and Schubert. The repertoire is so large and the stylistic variations so wide that it is of little value to comment on them here. In studying the piano you will play sonatas and smaller pieces by all these composers. But do not restrict yourself to the interpretation of the music; examine your pieces in detail and find out exactly how the sounds you hear have been set down on paper.

D. The composers for the piano of the nineteenth century romantic period: Schumann, Liszt, Chopin, Brahms, and many others. The technique of piano playing developed hand-in-hand with the mechanics of the instrument. These advances, added to a new outlook on the character and emotional expressiveness of music, emphasize the contrast between the romantic and classical styles. Compare an early sonata by Beethoven (before op. 27) with Schumann's 'Papillons' or a Waltz by Chopin. The differences, amongst others, lie in the form, the changed view on 'development', the presentation of melody, a wider harmonic and key range, and a revolution in the manner of setting down the notes. See Schumann's 'Kinderscenen', 'Carnaval',

' Novelletten '; selected preludes, waltzes and études of Chopin; Brahms's variations on a theme by Handel, op. 24, intermezzi and other pieces in opp. 116, 117, 118 and 119, and (for piano duet) the Liebeslieder Waltzes.

E. Debussy and Ravel. Impressionism, making new demands on the piano, carried keyboard technique yet a stage further. See Debussy's ' Deux Arabesques ', ' Suite Bergamasque ', ' Images ', Children's Corner, Préludes (books I and II), and (for piano duet)' Petite Suite'; Ravel's ' Pavane pour une infante défunte ', ' Jeux d'eau ', Sonatine, ' Le Tombeau de Couperin ', and (for piano duet) ' Ma Mère l'Oye '.

F. Finally, two composers nearer our own time must be chosen from the hundreds who, together, have produced a formidable repertoire: Bartók's ' For Children ', ' Out of Doors ', and Mikrokosmos (a most important series of graded pieces collected into six books); and Hindemith's ' Ludus Tonalis ' (described as ' studies in counterpoint, tonal organization and piano playing ').

3. Study closely some of the representative pieces mentioned above. Musical style is the outcome of aesthetic and social development or fashion; and each style employs its peculiar technique and chordal vocabulary. A student of music should be able to distinguish at sight between the principal periods of keyboard writing, in the same way that he should (by this stage in his course) be able to tell the difference between, say, a Bach chorale and a canzonet by Morley. In Chapter 34 you were asked to write a two-part invention; and you may have used one of Bach's inventions as a pattern. As you gain confidence you may begin to set down your ideas in the styles of other composers. To imitate the music of a past generation is a valuable training. But your eyes and ears must be continually open for the salient features which go to create style.

4. Sometimes you will be required to add a piano part below a vocal or instrumental line. Here, again, begin by imitating a style with which you are familiar. If it is to be the continuo part to a recitative, follow (say) the example of Handel (Fig. 368). Strict adherence to the laws of part-writing is not always possible, but those relating to parallel motion between extremes should be observed. It is also better to maintain a regular number of parts—three or four, as may be most suitable. A close position (as in the quotation from Handel) is satisfactory for recitative; but it is good practice to work more vocally in three or four parts, either for recitative or for the realization of the figured bass below a more melodic line (Figs. 501 and 502).

5. A piano part in combination with a solo line will, with advantage, alternate between several methods of expression. It is seldom good to maintain one pattern of texture for too long—as we have seen in writing for strings. Thus, Haydn (Fig. 495) presents three distinct patterns in the course of eight bars. In Fig. 493 he gives us only two

Fig. 501

—the striking rhythm of bars 1 and 5 alternating with the remainder. Examine the extract below[1] from a violin sonata. In this there are as many as five ideas (in the piano part) in eighteen bars; the character of each is clearly defined. Note that the chords contain a regular number of notes; when one hand plays broken chords the 'part writing' follows normal practice—sevenths falling, and so on.

Fig. 503

[1] Here the piano is equal in importance to the violin: its part is not an accompaniment (and therefore subordinate) to that of a solo instrument.

6. The manner of setting out the notes of a piano part on paper must often be a compromise between what is true and what is clear to the eye. The problem arises because a ' piano style ' has never rid itself completely of its vocal or consort origins. A passage which is, in essence, an upper melody, a bass line, and a central chordal pattern should be so set out that the eye can follow the progress of each separate unit. Among well known examples of this kind are the slow movement of Beethoven's piano sonata, op. 13 (compare bars 1-2 with 37-38); Chopin's preludes, op. 28, Nos. 6, 9 and others, as well as many passages in the nocturnes and études. The accompanimental framework may, if desired, be *arpeggiando* in outline (as in Nos. 15 and 25 of Mendelssohn's ' Songs Without Words '). But whatever the demands of the moment, make the part-writing clear to the eye and convenient to the hand. Compare the following; and study some song accompaniments (as in Schubert, Schumann, Brahms, Vaughan Williams, and others).

Fig. 504

Fig. 505

Fig. 506

Fig. 507

NOTES

1. Scales and Modes

The wide use of major and minor keys in music most generally heard in western countries today may give the impression that the two scales on which these keys are founded are the only ones in existence. That is not so. There have been, and there are still, many other scales. Those used in eastern countries are quite different from ours, and a totally different style of music results. Some of these oriental scales do not recognize the fundamental importance of the octave; others have a larger number of divisions within the octave—as many as twenty-two (Hindu) or twenty-four (Persian and Arabic); while the Japanese scale is pentatonic (composed of five degrees) with sub-divisions into semitones.

The two diatonic scales discussed in these volumes had their origin in the medieval system of Ecclesiastical modes. These modes, which had assumed their basic form not later than the end of the sixth century, were eight in number. The four odd-numbered modes (called ' authentic ') corresponded to an octave of the white notes of the piano beginning and ending on D (the Dorian mode), on E (Phrygian), on F (Lydian) and on G (Mixolydian). It will be seen (Fig. 508) that the order of tones and semitones is different in each of these modes; hence the fact that, whereas all major scales are alike in character, since the order of their component intervals is identical, no two modes can ever be alike.

It was customary to recite the principal portion of passages from the liturgy on (or around) a note one fifth above the first degree of the mode, with the result that this note assumed considerable importance and is known to us as the Dominant. The first degree, the origin of the mode, was also the cadence-point or resting place of the plainsong; we call it the Final. These two terms and the degrees to which they refer are important in considering the modes. (The dominant of the Phrygian mode was later changed from B to C for reasons which need not worry us at this point.) The melody in an authentic mode moved between the final and its octave, and concluded on the final.

Fig. 508

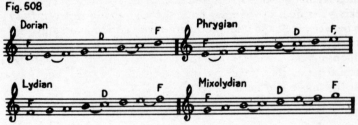

Towards the end of the sixth century Pope Gregory gave these four authentic modes a new (plagal) form by permitting the melody to range between the *dominant* and its octave; the final remained (in the middle) as the cadence-point.

Fig. 509

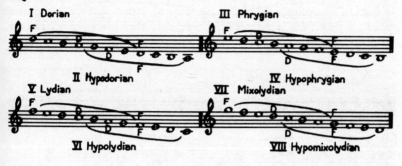

It was not until the middle of the sixteenth century that four additional modes were added, making twelve in all. Those with the final on A (the Aeolian) will be recognized as the original form of our modern minor scale; and those beginning on C (the Ionian) are similar to our major scale.

Fig. 510

Reference is occasionally made to modes XI and XII which are termed Locrian and Hypolocrian respectively—with their finals on B. These modes, existing only in theory, can be ignored: but they explain the usual numbering of the Ionian and Hypoionian as XIII and XIV —when only twelve modes are accepted.

Recognition by ear of the mode in which a melody is written is a skilled technique. But it can be calculated (with the aid of the eye) by seeking the final of the melody, and then looking to see if the range lies between final and final (authentic form) or dominant and dominant (plagal form). Melodies accompanied or worked out in true modal fashion should have no signature; the only transposition originally permitted was that involving the introduction of one flat, indicating that the music had been raised a fourth.

Study the following melodies and note the modes in which they are written.

Fig. 511

(Mixolydian)

Brennan on the Moor

(Hypoaeolian)

'I will give my love an apple'

(Phrygian)

'Farewell, my joy and heart'

(Dorian)

The Drunken Sailor

(Lydian)   Beethoven

With the introduction of *musica ficta*, whereby flattened leading notes were sharpened or sharpened sixths were flattened (see Chapter 6, para. 6), the destruction of the unique character of the individual

modes was begun and a step was taken which was to lead eventually
to the supremacy of the Ionian and the Aeolian and the adoption
of the modern major/minor key system. Too frequent an inclusion of
the flattened sixth in the Dorian mode will transform the scale into
that of the Aeolian mode. Similarly, the addition of a sharp to the
leading note of the Mixolydian mode will create the Ionian mode—
the modern major scale.

While the major/minor key system has predominated throughout
the western world since the seventeenth century, other scale-patterns
have had a varying influence on musical composition.

(a) The Pentatonic Scale:

In this scale there are only five notes to the octave; not equidistant,
but arranged with gaps. Any selection of notes can be made, though
in practice semitones are avoided (in Western usage) and the intervals
of the scale are usually arranged as T—T—minor 3rd—T—minor 3rd.

Many beautiful melodies are written on a pentatonic scale. In
addition to those quoted below there are such well-known tunes as
' Massa's in de cold, cold ground ' (Fig. 295) and ' Ye Banks and
Braes o' Bonnie Doon '.

(b) The Whole-Tone Scale:

Strictly, two scales consisting only of whole tones can be contained
in an octave—that beginning on C, and that on C♯. In practice, since
the exclusive use of only one of these possible scales would eliminate
half the notes in the octave, the complete scale is rarely adhered to.

It is more common to find melodic fragments which, beginning on any degree of the octave, proceed by whole tones. Thus, it is questionable whether such a series of notes can truly be termed a 'scale'. Two quotations illustrating the employment of whole-tone series are taken from Debussy's opera *Pelléas et Mélisande*. Glinka also experimented on these lines, and other nineteenth-century composers have included phrases built on a similar pattern.

Fig. 513

Lourd et sombre   Debussy

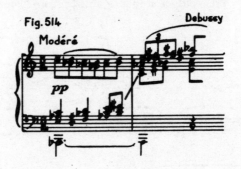

Fig. 514

Modéré   Debussy

2. Cadences

Cadence patterns have altered greatly since polyphonic music began to be practised some eleven centuries ago. One of the duties of the cadence has always been to lead a musical phrase or composition to a point of rest. Perfection of ending has been the aim of succeeding generations of composers; and, according to their view of musical aesthetics, they achieved that aim each in his own manner. So it is misleading to call the final progression from dominant to tonic 'the perfect' cadence, as if it is the only pattern which has ever fully satisfied the demands made of it. The term 'authentic', as applied to the cadence V–I, is to be preferred.

The cadential pattern which obtained throughout the period of medieval music was established on the descent by step of the tenor to the final of the mode. Above this the other part or parts moved by contrary motion to the octave of the final, or to the fifth (and perhaps to both).

Fig. 515

(tenor)

The composers of the middle ages held that the final chord of a passage should sound a perfect consonance—that is, a unison, an octave or a fifth; and, further, that the penultimate chord should sound an imperfect consonance—a sixth or a third (Chapter 4, para. 17). These conditions are fulfilled in the examples given in Fig. 515.

However firm the outlines of this pattern, ornamentation by suspension and auxiliaries was introduced freely (Fig. 516). Moreover, in the fourteenth century a variant of the medieval cadence became widespread, in which the leading note fell to the sixth of the mode before leaping to the final; it is sometimes referred to as the Landini sixth—though it was in use before the composer of that name flourished (1325–97) and even during his lifetime was not used exclusively by him (Fig. 517).

Fig. 516

French Discant (12th ©)   Worcester Motet Book (late 13th ©)

(meri) mor – tis ter – – mi – – num.

(re) me – – di – – – – um.

Fig. 517

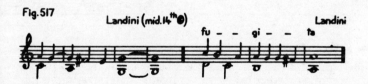

Landini (mid. 14th ©)   Landini

fu – – gi – – ta

It will be noticed that the medieval cadence is well suited to two- and three-part writing—indeed, we discussed it in Chapter 12 in connection with our own two-part writing. But when, on increasing the number of parts to four or five, a *bassus* was written below the tenor, there was a danger of interfering with the established pattern. The first solution was to interrupt the *bassus* during the cadential period and allow it to resume on the last note of all—after the remaining parts had sounded the medieval cadence in the normal manner. This could hardly be a permanent solution (Fig. 518). Next, the *bassus* was permitted to sound the dominant on the penultimate beat provided it did not proceed to double the tenor on the final but leapt an octave (or a sixth) to an inner part in the final chord (Fig. 519). This, again, was an unconvincing attempt to preserve the traditional pattern. So soon as the bass sounds the dominant on the penultimate beat the colour and character of the old cadence are partially dispersed and those of the (new) authentic cadence introduced, however vaguely, to the ear.

Fig. 518

Fig. 519

With the gradual decrease in importance of the tenor in favour of the bass, and the increased attention given to the top part, it was only a matter of time before the authentic took precedence over the medieval cadence. The leading note, by now usually raised by *musica ficta* to be a semitone below the final, was commonly introduced by a suspension; the tenor was freed from the obligation to descend to the final and could move to the third or elsewhere. The movement of the upper parts became more flexible, the new and important factor being the firm progress of the bass from dominant to final.

Fig. 520   Des Pres (early 16th ©)

Though the V–I close was often employed in its simplest form throughout the sixteenth century, the freedom of the individual parts made it the vehicle for many of the most beautiful cadences in musical history. The Tudor composers of England contributed their share of these graceful polyphonic endings; Figs. 522 and 523 are typical. And at Fig. 521 we have an example in which raised and flattened leading notes, each moving logically within its own part, conflict with exquisite effect. (It must be remembered that the discords in this quotation are intended to be sounded by voices; on the piano they are harsh.)

Fig. 521   Taverner (mid.16th ©)

Among other melodic decorations, the *nota cambiata* (Chapter 31) became a feature of the authentic cadence (Figs. 411–413).

Reference has already been made to the context in which the plagal cadence is most usually found—the continuation of the tonic (or final) as an inverted pedal after the sounding of an authentic close (Fig. 62). Many sixteenth-century works end with a plagal cadence alone; but the most common appearance of this pattern is after, and in conjunction with, the authentic form.

Fig. 522 — Byrd (c. 1600)

Fig. 523 — Taverner (mid. 16th C)

If the medieval close was unable to provide the most complete sense of perfection and rest sought in the sixteenth century, it continued as a passing or less emphatic cadence pattern. (Very often the upper parts were inverted, as at (l) and (m) in Fig. 524.)

Fig. 524 — Palestrina

et in u-num Do — mi-num Je — sum Chris-tum Fi-li-um De-i u-ni ge-ni-tum

The Phrygian cadence. The medieval close could be used in all modes. In all but the third mode the tenor descended a whole tone to the final; and it was the descent of only a *semitone* which gave special character to this cadence and linked it (as it still does today) with the Phrygian mode. When the medieval cadence was generally superseded in the sixteenth century, it was still impossible to build an authentic close (V–I) in the Phrygian mode; and so it became customary to use the medieval pattern (with bass descending a semitone to the final) as its authentic ending—hence the term Phrygian cadence.

The plagal form (IV–I) was also extensively used. Tallis's hymn-tune, 'Third Mode Melody' should be studied with regard to these two cadences (Fig. 526 and *English Hymnal*, No. 92).

In the Phrygian cadence we again see the effect of a change of outlook; the perfection of ending seems less secure to later generations. So much so that in the eighteenth century this cadence was frequently written as a formula of 'unrest': as a preparation for a new movement. In such contexts the cadence might be on the dominant or mediant of the tonality to follow, as in Fig. 527, and the well-known chords between the two movements of Bach's third Brandenburg concerto.

Fig. 525   Isaac

Fig. 526   Tallis

Fig. 527
Adagio   Allegro   Handel

Interrupted cadences. Throughout the early chapters of this Course we assumed that the interruption of an authentic close would be by a chord of the submediant (II–I$\frac{6}{4}$–V–VI), though it was stressed that any chord other than that of the tonic can, in theory, be a medium of interruption. A word must be said here on interruptions which not only prevent the sounding of the tonic but dispel the existing tonality and offer opportunities for settling in a new key. In Fig. 528 the interruption (a German sixth in G minor) is written out and treated as the dominant seventh of A♭. This could become a substantive modulation; but instead, the progression is continued through B♭ and C minor, and on to the Neapolitan sixth of G minor—and so back again to the cadence we expected fourteen bars earlier.

Fig. 528

A quotation from Wagner (Fig. 70) in Chapter 7 illustrated an interruption which, again, because of modulation, involved a long delay before the return to the original key. After reading Chapter 27 we recognize the chord on C♯ as a chromatic supertonic ninth (root omitted). This chord might have been used without disturbing the tonality of G major (Fig. 529); but Wagner chooses to convert the chromatic ninth into a (diatonic) ninth on the subdominant of E minor—and so moves away from the original key. Both these instances are extended interruptions; both of them, equally, show that an interruption can be made the point at which a substantive modulation is initiated.

Fig. 529

One of the most beautiful and ingenious uses of the formula of interruption occurs in the finale of Haydn's 'London' symphony. In leading back to the recapitulation there is an extended passage in F♯ minor. With a dynamic of *pp* a cadence in that key is interrupted by f♯VI—that is, by a chord of D major. The next moment we realize that f♯VI is being treated as DI—and that the recapitulation has begun unexpectedly. This is one of the great moments in music —and effected by the simplest means.

3. Figured Bass

We can think of figured bass as a musical short-hand to indicate quickly the nature of a chord on a bass, though without fixing the exact position of each note.

This system was developed, and its use became widespread, at the beginning of the seventeenth century. By it, the incomplete harmonies in compositions consisting of a bass and one or more upper parts were filled in by keyboard instruments; as, for instançe, in a violin sonata in which only the bass and the solo part were written out; or in recitative, where only the vocal line and the bass of the implied chords were given. Unlike the contrapuntal style of the sixteenth century, the music to which figured bass was applied was not complete as written in the score; the chords indicated by the figures were filled in on the organ, virginal or harpsichord at the discretion of the player. From about 1600 until well into the second half of the eighteenth century playing from figured bass was a necessary skill on the part of a well-trained musician.

To give the bass line substance, it was usually sustained by a cello, with or without a double bass. This combination of sustained bass line and keyboard extemporization was in certain circumstances termed *basso continuo*, and in others *thorough bass*. The definitions of these terms are outside our scope. But it should be mentioned that the continuo player (that is, the musician who read the figured bass at the keyboard) was often the leader of the ensemble, taking the place of our present-day conductor or organist.

As an example of the application of figured bass, compare the following quotation from an autograph manuscript of Handel's *Messiah* with the version printed in any modern edition. In the latter, the editor has filled in or (as we say) ' realized ' the figured bass according to his ideas of what the composer intended, taking the figures as his guide.

Fig. 531   Handel

His yoke_is_ ea — — — — — sy

6   6   6   6 5   6

The operas and oratorios of Handel and his contemporaries: the cantatas and settings of the ' Passion ' of J. S. Bach: the instrumental sonatas and ensembles of Purcell, Corelli, Vivaldi, and Telemann are among the wide range of works which, though seen today in ' realized ' editions, were originally figured.

By the first half of the eighteenth century the method of setting out the figures had become fairly standardized. A table of the signs suited for our own purpose is given below. Just as we put accidentals to the left of a note, so accidentals are best set to the left of the figure to which they refer—though some editions set them to the right. The third is usually indicated by an accidental alone; but the figure 3 can be added if confusion is likely to arise. 2 and 6 may be sharpened by an oblique stroke. 4 and 7 in many eighteenth-century scores, are sharpened by a vertical stroke to the bar: viz., 4+, 7: as this is some-times indistinct in manuscript, an accidental is to be recommended. An oblique stroke to the tail of 5 and 7 indicates a diminished interval: viz., 5̷, 7̷.

Fig. 532

♯2 or 2	♯ or ♯3	♯4, ♯, 4+	♯5	ᵗ or ♯6	♯7 or 7	♯9
♭2	♭ or ♭3	♭4	♭5	♭6	♭7	♭9
♮2	♮ or ♮3	♮4	♮5	♮6	♮7	♮9
			dimin.5̷		dimin.7̷	

As a short-hand in our own exercises, figuring may be assumed to be diatonic unless there is any special reason to the contrary. Thus at (l) below there is no need to indicate that the fifth of ⁶₅ is diminished. On the other hand, the chromatic nature of certain intervals at (m) must be made clear.

Fig. 533

(l)   (m)

6 9 —
5 7
   3 ♯

4+   6 7̷ ♭6 5—♭7 6—
2   ♮5 4 ♮—♭5

Short appoggiaturas may be left unfigured; and, if desired, some
passing notes. If there is room for doubt, figures should be inserted.

Abbreviations of the figuring of chords are referred to in the chapter
on the chord concerned. Thus, 7 standing for $\frac{7}{5}$, and $\frac{6}{3}$ for $\frac{6}{5}$ are
explained in Chapters 20 and 21.

4. Forbidden Consecutives

Fig.534

Sit glo — ri - a Do-mi- ni in sae-cu - la

Fig.535

Vaughan Williams

mi-se-re - re   no - bis

On seeing either of the above quotations in print you may wonder
why you, too, are not permitted to write consecutive fifths and octaves.
It is a question of style. Fig. 534 is an example of medieval organum
—parallel movement being the earliest form of polyphony. Fig. 535
is a quotation from the Mass in G minor by Vaughan Williams,
written about 1922. Each is ' correct ' according to the style in which
it is written.

Though organum was the style of the age in the ninth century,
developments in polyphony led (in the fourteenth century) to the
prohibition of parallel fifths and octaves. These intervals, sounded
consecutively, were no longer acceptable to the ear. This prohibition
remained generally intact until, towards the close of the nineteenth
century, consecutive fifths and octaves (as well as ninths and sevenths)
began to be introduced for special effect. Over the past fifty years
parallel intervals have become increasingly a part of the composer's
legitimate vocabulary and are no less ' correct ' than consecutive thirds
and sixths. Nevertheless, their effect is so marked that even today they
can only safely be used with discrimination.

Elementary courses in harmony and counterpoint are usually based
on musical styles stretching from the sixteenth to the early twentieth
centuries, and during those four hundred years parallel fifths and
octaves were avoided by all composers of repute. It was bad musical
grammar to transgress the laws of progression. On the other hand, the

use of consecutives in expressing an idiom of our own times is legitimate; though this is quite different from the sudden, over-looked, and un-calculated appearance of 'fifths' in a passage in which they are stylistically out of place.

The degree of movement of the parts necessary to avoid the effect of consecutives has altered at various times in musical history. Palestrina accepted the movement of one voice on the half-beat for this purpose (Fig. 536 (m)), in spite of the appearance of oblique octaves by so doing. Fifths at even closer quarters can be broken by a decorative pattern (l) and (o), or by an anticipation (n). In both these quotations the minim beats should be fast enough to give a flowing yet unhurried tempo.

Bach also, while observing the rules governing parallel motion, regarded movement on half-beats as sufficient to correct any sug-gestion of consecutives. If you compare the quotations by Palestrina with those by Bach below you will see that their views on this subject coincide closely. In the chorales, Bach's crotchets approximate in tempo to the minims in the examples from Palestrina. Bach, it will be noted, accepts the oblique 'fifths' in Fig. 540. And we have seen from Fig. 287 that he occasionally accepts consecutives created by the logical movements of the parts, in the same way that Purcell did (Fig. 288).

Fig. 538

Fig. 539

Fig. 540

5. Time-Signatures

Though the time-signatures set out in Chapter 8 (Fig. 88) are those normally used, such a list is far from complete. Since the later years of the nineteenth century composers have used other signatures, particularly 5 and 7, to break up the squareness of duple or the regular lilt of triple times. One of the well-known examples of $\frac{5}{4}$ occurs in Tchaikowsky's ' Pathetic ' Symphony.

Fig. 541

Allegro con grazia

Tchaikowsky

However indeterminate the rhythm of an irregular time, it is always divisible into simple units. The example from Tchaikowsky is basically 2+3. We can tell this from the phrasing, and from the second and fourth bars which are written ♩♩♩. and not ♩♩♩♩. The whole movement maintains this sub-division of the bar. In Holst's ' Mars ', while the principal theme is 3+2 (Fig. 542 (l)), a second theme begins with a rhythm of 2+3 and is then extended to 2+2+1⌣1+2+2 (m). These are typical of the varying shapes offered by such irregular time-signatures as 5 or 7 or 11.

Fig. 542

Because of the possibility of confusion, some composers indicate the multiples of these complex bars. This is especially helpful if, for instance, 4+3 is reversed to 3+4 for a few bars before resuming its original pattern.

Fig. 543

During the sixteenth century there was almost greater rhythmic freedom within the established time than today. The proper understanding of some madrigalian music is dependent on detecting where modifications to the basic rhythm are called for—though no change of time is indicated. An example is given at Fig. 546: if an accent is given to the first note in each bar the rhythm of the words is hampered. But if the same phrase is sung as set out at Fig. 547, both words and music fit perfectly. The re-arrangement of two bars of $\frac{3}{4}$ into one of $\frac{3}{2}$ is an example of what is called *hemiola*. More often (especially in the eighteenth century) cadences in triple time are treated in the same manner (Fig. 548).

Fig. 546

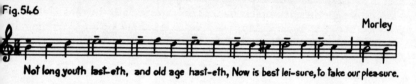

Not long youth last-eth, and old age hast-eth, Now is best lei-sure, to take our plea-sure.

Fig. 547

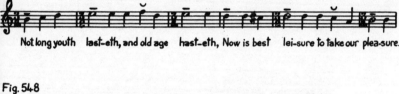

Not long youth last-eth, and old age hast-eth, Now is best lei-sure to take our plea-sure.

Fig. 548

DICTATION EXERCISES
(Chapters 10-21)

Chapter 10—Primary Triads

—*Primary and Secondary Triads*

Chapter 11

Chapter 12

Chapter 13

Chapter 14

(vii)

(viii)

Chapter 15

(i)

(ii)

(iii)

(iv)

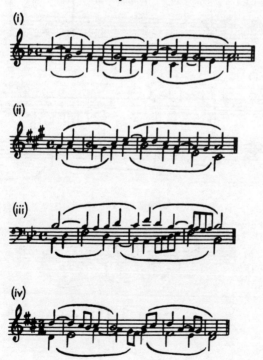

(v)

(vi)

(vii)

(viii)

Chapter 16

(i)

(ii)

(iii)

(iv)

(v)

Chapter 17

(i)

(ii)

(iii)

(iv)

Chapter 20

(i)

(ii)

(iii)

(iv)

Chapter 21

INDEX OF QUOTATIONS

ABT, F.
363   'The Wishing Well'
ASTON, HUGH
519   Missa, Te Deum (Agnus Dei)
BACH, J. S.
316   Chorale, 'Innsbruck' ('Nun ruhen alle Wälder')
321   St. Matthew Passion, No. 15
337   Fantasia (and fugue) in G minor for organ
359   Chorale, 'Liebster Gott, wann werd' ich sterben'
360   Chorale, 'Vater unser im Himmelreich'
366   Fantasia in G major for organ
367   (Passacaglia and) Fugue for organ
392   English Suite in A minor for harpsichord (Sarabande)
398   (Prelude and) Fugue for organ (The 'Dorian')
400   (Toccata and) Fugue for organ in D minor
408   Chorale, 'Nun danket alle Gott'
415   The St. Matthew Passion, No. 56
421   Prelude (and Fugue) in C minor for organ
422   Italian Concerto for harpsichord (slow mvt.)
423   Prelude (and Fugue) in D, Bk. I, '48'
444   Concerto in D minor for two violins (slow mvt.)
453   Prelude (and Fugue) in C minor for organ
465   Invention for harpsichord in C
466   Invention for harpsichord in D minor
467   (i) Fugue in G for organ
      (ii) (Prelude and) Fugue in D sharp minor, Bk. I, '48'
      (iii) (Prelude and) Fugue in A flat, Bk. I, '48'
      (Chorales)
470   'Freu' dich sehr, o meine Seele'
471   'Nun freut euch, lieben Christen'
472   'Gott hat das Evangelium'
473   'Von Gott will ich nicht lassen'
474   'Dank sei Gott in der Höhe'
475   'Gott des Himmels und der Erden'
476   'Ach Gott, wie manches Herzeleid'
477   'Kyrie, Gott Vater'
478   'Christum wir sollen loben schon'

479   'Herzlich thut mich verlangen'
480   'Es spricht der Unweisen Mund wohl'
481   'Ach, lieben Christen, seid getrost'
482   'Nun lasst uns Gott, dem Herren'
Chap. 35 Ex. 2 (Chorales)
      (i) 'O Lamm Gottes'
      (ii) 'Meinem Jesum lass' ich nicht'
      (iii) 'Was mein Gott will'
      (iv) 'Nun lasst uns Gott'
      (v) 'Herr Jesu Christ'
      (vi) 'Mach's mit mir, Gott'
      (vii) 'Wo soll ich fliehen hin?'
      (viii) 'Es ist gewisslich'
Chap. 35 Ex. 3 (Chorales)
      (i) 'Das alte Jahr'
      (ii) 'O Gott, du frommer Gott'
      (iii) 'Herzlich lieb hab' ich'
      (iv) 'Christ lag in Todesbanden'
490   Christmas Oratorio (Part II, Sinfonia)
528   Toccata (and Fugue) in F for organ

BARTÓK, B.
512   Mikrokosmos, Vol. IV, 105
544   Mikrokosmos, Vol. VI, 151

BEETHOVEN, L.
326   'Eroica' Symphony (slow mvt. bar 242)
331   'Eroica' Symphony (slow mvt. bar 4)
339   Symphony No. 1 in C (Finale, bar 207)
351   Fidelio, Overture
352   Piano Sonata, op. 10 No. 1
357   Piano Sonata, op. 26 (Variations)
369   Piano Trio in C minor, op. 1 No. 3 (1st mvt.)
376   Symphony No. 2 in D, op. 36 (1st mvt.)
382   Overture, Men of Prometheus
390   Symphony No. 4 in B flat, op. 60 (1st mvt., bar 291)
417   String Quartet in A flat, op. 74 (slow mvt.)
424   Piano Sonata, op. 2 No. 3 (Scherzo)
428   Piano Trio in C minor, op. 1 No. 3 (slow mvt.)
Chap. 32 Ex. 1 (iii) Waltz in F (Trio

BEETHOVEN, L.—Contd.
484 Violin Concerto in D (1st mvt.)
497(iv) String Quartet in F, op. 18 No. 1 (slow mvt.)
511 String Quartet in A minor, op. 132 (3rd mvt.)

BENNET, JOHN
413 Madrigal, 'All creatures now'

BIZET, G.
329 ⎱ Suite, *L'Arlésienne (Adagietto)*
354 ⎰

BRAHMS, J.
358 Motet, 'Wherefore now hath life', op. 74 No. 1
370 *Requiem*, No. 1
393 Festival Sentences, op. 109 (No. 2)
401/2 Intermezzo for piano, op. 119 No. 1
430 Liebeslieder Waltzes, 1st Set, No. 1
Chap. 31 Ex. 3 (iv) Chorale Prelude for Organ, 'Est ist ein Ros' '
441 String Sextet in B♭, op. 18 (1st mvt.)
445 *Requiem*, No. 7
507 'Sonntag'
545 Variations for piano on Hungarian Song, op. 21 No. 2

BYRD, WILLIAM
487/8 Fantasia for string sextet, 1611
498 Variation (No. 2) on 'Goe from my windoe', for virginal
499 'The Queenes Alman', for virginal
522 Short Service (Venite)

CORELLI, A.
317 Trio Sonata in E, op. 4 No. 6 (Giga)

DEBUSSY, C.
497(v) String Quartet (2nd mvt.)
513 *Pelléas et Mélisande*, (p. 142 vocal score)
514 *Pelléas et Mélisande* (p. 260 vocal score)

GIBBONS, ORLANDO
323(iii) 'Song 67'

GREENE, MAURICE
501 Anthem, 'My God, my God'

HANDEL, G. F.
368 *Messiah*, No. 29
383 *Messiah*, No. 46
404 *Messiah*, No. 5
405 *Messiah*, No. 12
407 Harpsichord Suite in G, No. XIV (Air)
491 Concerto Grosso in D minor, op. 10 (Finale)

500 Harpsichord Suite in G minor, No. IX (Allemande)
527 Organ concerto in G minor
531 *Messiah*, No. 21
548 Concerto Grosso in E minor, op. 6 No. 3

HAYDN, J.
396 Piano Sonata in E (Finale)
397 Piano Sonata in D (Largo)
410 Symphony in G, No. 94 (1st mvt.)
418 String Quartet in C, op. 54 No. 2 (1st mvt.)
425 Piano Sonata in D (1st mvt.)
440 Symphony in G, No. 94 (Slow mvt.)
493 String Quartet in D, op. 76, No. 5 (1st mvt.)
495 String Quartet in E flat, op. 33, No. 2 (1st mvt.)
530 Symphony in D (The 'London') (Finale, bar 191)

HOLST, G.
542 *The Planets*, Mars
543 *Rig Veda* Hymns, 1st Group (Funeral Hymn)

HUNT, THOMAS
399 Madrigal, 'Hark! did you ever hear?'

HYMN TUNES
323(iii) 'Song 67'
343 'Wareham'
526 Tallis's Third Mode Melody

LA RUE, P. DE
Chap 34 Ex. 1 (i) Missa, De beata Virgine

MENDELSSOHN-BARTHOLDY, F
381 Scottish Symphony (Scherzo)
426 'Songs without Words', No. 30
506 'Songs without Words', No. 18

MORLEY, THOMAS
460/2 Canzonet, 'Lo here another love'
463 Canzonet, 'Deep lamenting'
464 Canzonet, 'Where art thou, wanton'
546/7 Ballet, 'Sing we and chant it'

MOZART, W. A.
338 Piano Sonata in F, K. 332
356 String Quartet in B♭, K. 458 (Trio)
386 Symphony in C, K. 551 (Finale, bar 219)
406 String Quartet in B flat, K. 458 (1st mvt.)
431 Symphony in D, K. 504 (Slow mvt.)
433 Symphony in G minor, K. 550 (Finale, bar 71)
Chap. 31 Ex. 3 (iii) Six German Dances, K. 600, No. 1

Mozart, W. A.—Contd.
Chap. 32 Ex. 1
    (i) Sinfonia Concertante, K. 364 (3rd mvt. bar 80)
    (ii) Sinfonia Concertante, K. 364 (2nd mvt.)
458 String Quartet in D, K. 575 (1st mvt. bar 49)
496 String Quartet in C, K. 465 (Slow mvt.)
497(i) String Quintet in G minor, K. 516 (Finale)
503 Sonata for piano and violin in F, K. 376 (1st mvt.)

Ockeghem, J.
518 Missa Caput (Kyrie)

Palestrina, G. P.
412 Missa, Papae Marcelli (Qui sedes)
414 Missa, Papae Marcelli (Qui venit)
524 Missa, Papae Marcelli (Credo)
536 Missa, Assumpta est Maria (Kyrie)
537 Motet, Tu es Pastor ovium

Purcell, Henry
409 Anthem, 'Praise the Lord, O my soul'
416 *Dido and Aeneas*
489 *King Arthur* (Hornpipe)

Rheinberger, J. G.
384 Organ Sonata in F sharp, op. 111 (Finale)
385 Organ Sonata in F sharp, op. 111 (2nd mvt.)
387 Organ sonata in F sharp, op. 111 (2nd mvt.)

Saint-Saëns, C.
388 *Danse Macabre* (M–N)

Schubert, F.
327 Symphony No. 9 in C (1st mvt.)
353 String Quartet in D minor (Variations)
377 String Quintet in C (Slow mvt.)
443 'Whither' (from *The Maid of the Mill*)
485 String Quartet in D minor (1st mvt.)

497(ii) Octet, op. 166 (4th mvt.)
    (iii) String Quartet Movement in C minor

Schumann, R.
Chap. 32 Ex. 1 (iv) Sonata for the Young, No. 1 (Doll's Cradle Song)
Chap. 32 Ex. 1 (v) Album Leaves, No. 5
504 *Papillons*, No. 7
505 *Papillons*, No. 10

Tallis, Thomas
526 'Third Mode Melody'

Taverner, John
521 Te Deum
523 Mass, In all devotion (Gloria)

Tchaikowsky, P.
541 Symphony No. 6 (Pathétique), op. 74 (2nd mvt.)

Telemann, G. P.
502 Trio Sonata for flute and violin

Tomkins, Thomas
Chap. 34 Ex. 3 (iii) Song, ' Love cease tormenting' (1622)

Vaughan Williams, R.
535 Mass in G minor (Gloria)

Verdi, G.
348/9 *Requiem* (Recordare)
350 *Otello*, Act III, vii

Vittoria, T.
Chap. 34 Ex. 1 (ii) Responsory, Amicus meus

Wagner, R.
340 *The Valkyrie*, Act I, i
341 *The Twilight of the Gods*, Act III, ii
347 *The Mastersingers*, Act I, iii
389 *The Valkyrie*, Act II, iv
395 *Parsifal*, Act I
427 *The Mastersingers*, Act III, v ('Prize Song')
432 *Tristan and Isolde*, Prelude

Weelkes, Thomas
Chap. 34 Ex. 3 (i) Air, 'Say wanton will you love me?' (1608)
Chap. 34 Ex. 3 (ii) Madrigal, 'My flocks feed not' (1597)